The Rajneesh Papers
STUDIES IN A NEW RELIGIOUS MOVEMENT

The Rajneesh Papers
Studies in a New Religious Movement

SUSAN J. PALMER
ARVIND SHARMA

MOTILAL BANARSIDASS PUBLISHERS
PRIVATE LIMITED • DELHI

First Edition : Delhi, 1993

© MOTILAL BANARSIDASS PUBLISHERS PRIVATE LIMITED
All Rights Reserved

ISBN: 81-208-1080-5

Also available at:
MOTILAL BANARSIDASS
41 U.A. Bungalow Road, Jawahar Nagar, Delhi 110 007
120 Royapettah High Road, Mylapore, Madras 600 004
16 St. Mark's Road, Bangalore 560 001
Ashok Rajpath, Patna 800 004
Chowk, Varanasi 221 001

PRINTED IN INDIA
BY JAINENDRA PRAKASH JAIN AT SHRI JAINENDRA PRESS,
A-45 NARAINA INDUSTRIAL AREA, PHASE I, NEW DELHI 110 028
AND PUBLISHED BY NARENDRA PRAKASH JAIN FOR MOTILAL
BANARSIDASS PUBLISHERS PVT. LTD., BUNGALOW ROAD,
JAWAHAR NAGAR, DELHI 110 007

CONTENTS

Editor's Note	vii
Acknowledgements	ix
Introduction SUSAN J. PALMER	xi
1. Rajneesh and the Guru Tradition in India ARVIND SHARMA	1
2. The Crazies—Who Follows Rajneesh and Why TED MANN	17
3. The Work of Osho Rajneesh: A Thematic Overview SWAMI ANAND JINA	47
4. Therapeutic Aspects of New Religious Movements FREDERICK BIRD and ROOSHIKUMAR PANDYA	57
5. The Meaning of Discipleship: Interview with a Rajneesh Therapist, Swami Veet Atito SUSAN J. PALMER	85
6. Rajneesh Women: Lovers and Leaders in a Utopian Commune SUSAN J. PALMER	103
7. A Letter from Poona, November, 1989 JAMES S. GORDON	137
Epilogue ARVIND SHARMA and SUSAN J. PALMER	155
Afterword SWAMI SATYA VEDANT (VASANT JOSHI)	163
Postscript	167
Contributors	169
Bibliography	171
References	179
Glossary	185
Index	187

EDITOR'S NOTE

Since the name of the movement and the title of its leader has changed intermittently, the use of proper names, titles, and "Rajneeshese" which might otherwise appear to be haphazard or inconsistent in this work, requires some explanation. Most scholars refer to the leader-founder as "Rajneesh", his legal name. His spiritual titles are tried on and discarded like masks. Moreover, the use of these titles implies a devotional stance inappropriate in a researcher. The movement became incorporated in the mid-70's as the *Rajneesh Foundation International*. During the decline of Rajneeshpuram in late 1985, the name was changed to *Rajneesh Friends International*, a sign of Rajneesh's attempt to de*institutionalize his organization. The religion created by Rajneesh was labelled "Rajneeshism" in 1982. Sannyasins were told to refer to themselves as "Rajneeshee" in order to present a church-like facade to the IRS. Rajneesh abolished "Rajneeshism" in September, 1985. The correct term for a disciple is *sannyasin*, meaning one who has be initiated into "neo-sannyas". Sannyasins today find the out-of-date use of the term "Rajneeshee" intensely irritating. The women are titled "Ma", the men "Swami".

ACKNOWLEDGEMENTS

The editors would like to thank Ma Dhyan Usha for typing this manuscript and for keeping us in touch with the movement. Also, we are very grateful to the sannyasins in Australia and Canada who have shared their understandings of their Master's work and energy with us.

INTRODUCTION

Susan J. Palmer

The *Symposium on the Rajneesh Movement* was held on May 20, 1989 at the Faculty of Religious Studies of McGill University. This event came about as the result of a conversation between myself and Dr. Arvind Sharma. While sipping symposium tea in styrofoam cups at the "Triple SR" meeting in Chicago, we discovered we shared a common interest—we were both "Rajneesh watchers."

Through attending learned conferences I had recently become aware of the existence of a network of scholars (many of them ordained ministers) who unabashedly describe themselves as "Moon watchers". These enthusiasts, who are dotted about the North American continent, collect and exchange the unedited sermons of Reverend Moon, and file clippings on the latest court battles, deprogrammings, and other indignities suffered by the "Moonies." Having met Dr. Sharma, I began to hope a similar network might form around my favourite guru.

My fascination for the enigmatic Acharya-Bhagwan-Buddha-Osho Rajneesh whose frequent title changes reflect the divagations in his leadership, originated five years ago when the Rajneesh Meditation Centre/Cafe opened on my street. At this time the only people who shared my interest were the disciples themselves. While bowled over by Bhagwan's charm, I somehow managed to remain (perversely, as far as the disciples were concerned) impervious to "His" charisma. Meanwhile, unbeknownst to me, in early 1986, as I was observing the disbanding of the Rajneesh commune in Montreal, Dr. Sharma was studying the commune in Sydney, Australia. This was also abandoning its communal ideals and in the wake of Rajneeshpuram's collapse was placing a new emphasis on individuality. When I mentioned that I had recently been in contact with Dr. Edward Mann in Toronto, whose research into the Rajneesh spanned a decade and included interviews with the "supermoms" and "power ladies," it occurred to us that there might be enough Rajneesh watchers in Canada to hold a symposium.

Besides inviting the participation of prominent scholars in the Hindu tradition such as Dr. Robert Gussner of the University of Vermont and Dr. Katherine Young of McGill University, we decided to ask the local neo-sannyasins to present their own version of their movement. This put us, the "watchers" in the rather uncomfortable position of being watched by those who had surrendered to Rajneesh. The fruit of our watching was now to be weighed and evaluated by the former objects of our scrutiny. This confrontation between two apparently incompatible points of view proved stimulating, (at times *too* stimulating for me, the co-chairperson), particularly so because Rajneesh disciples, as former inmates of an ongoing therapy group that was the commune, are adept in the confrontational techniques of encounter.

In choosing to hold a symposium in which both scholars and sannyasins participated, Dr. Sharma and I were (perhaps selfconsciously) adding a new wrinkle to the increasingly convoluted relationship between sociologists and the new religions. In recent years it has become an established pattern for some movements to eagerly recruit scholars to study them. Tom Robbins has dubbed this phenomenon "philomandarinism" (Robbins, 1988). The Unification Church, for example, has organized conferences in exotic locations in which scholars have had their expenses paid and their papers published. The extrinsic credibility of these "kept scholars" (Robbins again) or putatively "coopted" academics has accordingly suffered. In the case of our symposium, however, it was the scholars who courted the spiritual seekers. This task fell to me, and it was not an easy one. Unlike the "Moonies" and the "Hare Krishna," the Rajneeshee, as a rule, are not eager to be studied. Far from adopting a "philomandarin" pose, they could be considered "mandarinphobic." Their lack of reverence of scholarship, in fact, had been one of the major obstacles in my own research efforts. There appear to be three reasons for their disdain for academia.

Introduction

First, the Rajneeshee, unlike the Hare Krishna or the Unification Church, are not evangelists. They do not have a missionary program. Far from trying to impose their beliefs on others, sannyasins, (or at least the ones I interviewed), claim to have "no beliefs". As I become better acquainted with them, however, I realized that they did share common beliefs, if only the belief they had no beliefs. Secondly, members tend to be from the middle to upper-middle class intelligentsia and are highly educated. As former participants in the Human Potential Movement, currently engaged in "body-work" or "energy-work," they tend to exhibit the kind of anti-intellectualism found only among intellectuals. Thirdly, the Rajneeshee in Montreal appear to be indifferent to their public image, and to lack a Public Relations department. When I first approached the members of the Montreal commune in 1984 with aspirations to study them, I was surprised to find that they presented no united front. They appeared to consider my research efforts so insignificant that they did not bother to discuss me among themselves. This was a very different situation from that which I had encountered in the local Krishna Temple and Unification Centre. I was forced to approach each sannyasin individually and request an interview, and received a bewildering variety of idiosyncratic responses.

The papers published in this volume, therefore, reflect the nature of the symposium, which, while intended to be a dialogue between scholars and spiritual seekers, perhaps dramatizes the differences between these diametrically opposed perspectives. Seekers can admit the veracity and fairness of an academic study of their religion, but the interpretation will always strike them as irrelevant and depressingly secular. Scholars can enrich their understanding of the subject by trying to absorb the subtleties of the informant's experience, but in the end they will imprison it within the grid of their own categories. We were fortunate to have two participants in the symposium who are both academics and initiated disciples of Rajneesh, and were useful facilitators in the moments "stuck energy" (to use a Rajneeshee term). These two are Dr. Jack Rains (Swami Veet Atito) and Dr. Robert Gussner (Swami Anand Jina) whose experience with Rajneesh is described in their papers.

As accounts of this NRM's history suggest, it is not an easy task to analyze this complex and chameleon-like religion. Carter, in his 1987 study of Rajneeshpuram, notes that "Special problems are posed by the dispersal, rapid changes, adapting to external constraints, and contact management of the new religions." He stresses the particular difficulties confronting the researcher who tries to "make sense" out of the Rajneesh:

> With the Rajneesh it is especially difficult to locate the movement 1) in physical space and time; 2) in terms of formal and legal structures; and 3) in terms of ideology and historical-cultural perspective:...the Rajneesh illustrate the research problems well, in that they are unusually mobile, legally creative and ideologically heterodox (Carter, 1987).

While there are, many aspects of Rajneeshism worthy of study, this volume focusses on the following issues: Rajneesh's leadership, the therapeutic benefits of meditation, the internal politics and social organization of Rajneeshpuram, gender roles in a utopian commune, and the psychological impact of conversion and initiation. In order to understand what these papers contribute to "Rajneesh studies" it would be useful to review the academic, and quasi-academic literature on Rajneesh and his movement which has appeared in the last five years.

A Review of the Literature

Unlike other large, conspicuously clothed and/or controversial "cults" such as the "Hare Krishna", the "Moonies" and the Scientologists, who have received extensive attention from scholars (Johnson, 1974; Shinn, 1987; Barker, 1985; Wallis, 1977), the Rajneesh have been virtually ignored until the dramatic fall of Rajneeshpuram. The well-publicized "Sheela scandal" stimulated a proliferation of journalists' accounts of Bhagwan's trials and a few academic studies of the movement, which suggests this might be another instance of sociologists receiving their problem focus from the media. The more useful works fall into 3 categories.

The first detailed studies of the Rajneesh were semi-autobiographical travelogues by journalists and novelists. These include *Flowers of Emptiness* by Sally Belfrage (1984) which describes her visit to the ashram in Poona and her short-lived initiation. *Rajneeshpuram: The Unwelcome Society* was written by a journalist who interviewed leaders in Rajneeshpuram, and evidently found the atmosphere of sexual permissiveness inspiring (Braun, 1984). Two years later the well-known *New Yorker* article by Frances Fitzgerald appeared, which received an interesting review in the *Rajneesh Times*. While the staff in Rajneeshpuram were evidently flattered that the grand-daughter of F. Scott (and a Pulitzer prize winner at that) should choose them for a piece in the prestigious *New Yorker*, they strongly disagree with her theory that Rajneesh has a martyr complex, and seemed rather hurt that, after all the "growth movement hugs" they had bestowed upon her, she should have the temerity to snicker at their therapy (e.g. "The place was awash in the Human Potential Movement"). Besides these generally intelligent and thoughtful works there were, of course, many entertaining pieces of journalism which cited useful and often carefully-researched facts and figures concerning the group's fund-raising activities and legal battles (*Oregonian*, June 1985; *Penthouse*, July 1985), but which ignored the group's religious life and spiritual appeal.

The second category of work is the biographical accounts of their years in the movement by apostates. These began finding willing publishers shortly after the collapse of Rajneeshpuram. For sannyasins, the most objectionable of these is Hugh Milne's *Bhagwan, the God That Failed* (1986), which is a (not altogether) hostile internalist's account of his erratic career as Bhagwan's "personal bodyguard". It offers the reader vivid descriptions of the politics and lifestyle of the core group surrounding Bhagwan, and Milne manifests a broad grasp of the movement's growth and changing directions. It is not exactly an objective report, since the author is obviously driven by a need to make moral sense—and publishing profit—out of a ten-year association which left him embittered, disoriented, and impoverished. Moveover, the book is somewhat marred by a certain sensationalism. There is more than a hint of *machismo* in the author's tendency to boast about his sexual conquests and in the rather caddish put-downs of sexual performances of friends and lovers. Sheela he dismisses as "frigid", (a very serious accusation in the Rajneesh culture). He even dares to cast doubt on the prowess of the "sex guru" himself. Nevertheless, aside from these defects (or assets for the schlockmeister-publisher), his book appears to be an honest attempt at "spiritual biography." At least Milne avoids the tendency, often found in apostates' accounts, to dehumanize fellow members and present them as "victims of some routinely effective and ineluctable technology of mind control" (Wallis, 1985:134).

Dr. George Meredith's book, *Bhagwan: The Most Godless Yet the Most Godly Man*, which appeared a year later, is evidently motivated by a desire to correct Milne's bad image of the group. Chapter 21 is devoted to pointing out factual errors and correcting distortions in Milne's book and winds up with a Freudian psychoanalytical, *ad hominum* attack on Milne. Meredith, one of the major doctors in the ashram's clinic, focuses particularly on refuting Milne's picture of a community rife with STD and malnutrition, and as Rajneesh's physician he is entitled to defend his reputation. He also claims that Milne grossly inflates his own status in the group; that he was never Bhagwan's "personal bodyguard," merely a bodyguard. To what extent Milne was a member of the "inner circle" is of course impossible for an outsider to judge.

Oddly enough, Meredith does not comment on Milne's most damaging onslaught: his anecdote—which might have been lifted from *Mary Poppins*—of Bhagwan "high" on laughing gas and giggling in his fancy dentist chair.

If Milne's account is suspect because he is hostile, Meredith's cannot be regarded as truly objective because he is more than "sympathetic", his tone is intensely devotional. Nevertheless, this particular reader was inclined to trust Meredith's version rather than Milne's because it was more intelligent, in better taste, and superior in its literary style (not that these constitute reliable criteria of veracity).

The third category is the small, but rapidly expanding, body of work on the Rajneesh in the microsociology of new religions. Roy Wallis' "Religion as Fun" (1987), contains a very useful survey of the professional and social background of members,

Introduction   xvii

and a daring but coherent summary of Rajneesh's thought. Since the leader is perhaps the most taped and videotaped man in history and, moreover, appears to take pride in his paradoxical utterances, abrupt philosophical *volte faces*, flat contradictions of previous statements, and mysterious warnings concerning the ineffable nature of religious experience, this is a no mean undertaking.

Two articles on the movement in America have appeared in learned journals. Lewis Carter's "The New Renunciates of Bhagwan Shree Rajneesh," is the result of an extensive research project of the Sociology Department of Washington State University on the 4,000 odd members living in Rajneeshpuram. It conveys the complexity and diffuse nature of this organization and is concerned more with describing the methodological problems this poses for the researcher than with trying to paint a coherent portrait of a religion. It contains some jarring references to "The Bhagwan," even in quoted interviews with disciples. This sounds as incongruous as a born-again Christian praying to "the Jesus."

"Charisma and Abdication: A Study of the Leadership of Bhagwan Shree Rajneesh" by Susan J. Palmer appeared in *Sociological Analysis* in 1988. Since it would be inappropriate to review my own article, I will quote the *Rajneesh Times* summary of its content:

> ...In the present study she is interested in "charismatic religious leadership" and specifically in the "living leader's struggle to keep his or her charismatic authority untrammelled by the forces of institutionalization." To this end, she studied the history of Rajneeshpuram, and attempted to apply the existing body of social theory, developed by Roy Wallis of The Queen's University, Belfast. This theory considers that the seemingly erratic behaviour by a charismatic leader has the purpose of breaking up "bureau-cratization and traditionalization" among his followers, which enhances his own direct control of them (*Rajneesh Times*, June 1, 1989).

The Golden Guru (1986) by James Gordon is a vivid account of the author's involvement in the movement both as a psychologist assessing the therapeutic benefits of Dynamic Meditation, and as a spiritual seeker. Gordon has the advantage of a close acquaintance with many of the leaders and the ability to "fit in," so that he evidently inspired confidence, although he never "took sannyas." Although this book is not a work of sociology, it does, however, contain many insights and descriptive passages useful for the sociologist of religion. As a seeker and "third force" psychologist, Gordon is concerned with the question of Rajneesh's enlightenment: was he once enlightened and, if so, did he "lose it"? The last chapter presents a powerful argument for Rajneesh's complicity in Sheela's crimes. While his case is very convincing, it is, for lack of available documentary evidence, ultimately no more that an hunch.

"The Rajneesh Movement" by Arvind Sharma which appears in *Genesis Exodus, and Numbers* (Stark 1985), is a precise and thoughtful description of the Poona community, which he visited in 1979. It was written for a 1982 meeting of sociologists interested in the new religions, who were still unfamiliar with this Indian-based NRM. Besides providing an historical account of Rajneesh's early career, Sharma raises some important questions concerning the psychological and spiritual effects of the peculiar mixture of eastern meditations with psychotherapeutic techniques on disciples following Rajneesh's *sadhana*. Does the cathartic technique of Dynamic Meditation merely "raise mud that will sink to the bottom again"? Does the groups' emphasis on psyche rather than soul represent a despiritualization of Hinduism? While other writers and former disciples have raised doubts concerning Rajneesh's claim to be an enlightened master, this is the only attempt to examine the model of the *atman* and the theory behind the meditation practice in Rajneesh's system: it notes the ways in which Rajneeshism departs from traditional models of Hindu philosophy and practice and raises the question "how effective is it?"

The Rajneesh Papers

The six essays included in this volume reflect the complexity of Rajneesh's movement: its geographical dislocations, its syncretism of eastern meditation and eastern psychotherapy; the waxing and waning of its communal phase with the corresponding rise and decline (and ensuing reconstruction) of commitment.

These different phases and facets of the movement are explored. The opening paper by Arvind Sharma investigates the *modus operandi* of Rajneesh's leadership by attempting to place his within a typology of the guru tradition in India. This fills an important vacuum, for (as far as I am aware) the relatively modest body of Rajneesh studies are all concerned with his significance in the West. Moon watchers meet the same obstacle: there are no reliable studies of the early days of Unificationism in Korea. The second essay is a study of "who joins . . . and why" by Ted Mann, in which he summarizes the prevailing research on membership in the movement, and classifies the different groups of people who are attracted to Rajneesh, in terms of their social background and profession.

Robert Gussner's account of his movement's history represents a sympathetic insider's point of view. The set of events leading to the fall of Rajneeshpuram are explained in this account as the external manifestations of an inner, spiritual process: the *sadhana* which Rajneesh lays out for his disciples. In this way, Dr. Gussner provides the reader with a coherent picture of the different phases of Rajneesh's "work" while the ups and downs of the organization are seen as inevitable responses to an increasingly hostile host society.

The papers written by Bird and Pandya are the result of research into the Rajneesh community in Montreal. Frederick Bird and Rooshikumar Pandya employ quantitative methods to compare the therapeutic benefits derived from involvement in the local Rajneesh group to those derived from three other groups: Transactional Analysis, Creative Awareness, and a control group. This study was conducted in 1981 during the first burst of Rajneeshee communal fervour, and therefore the tendency noted by Bird and Pandya of sannyasins to withdraw from institutions and family ties perhaps reflects the sectarian attitudes fostered during this commune building phase.

The sixth paper is in the form of an interview in which Jack Rains describes his visit to the Poona ashram in 1979 and his subsequent initiation into "neo-sannyas." This account offers the reader some insights into the conversion experience and the meaning of discipleship and explores the therapeutic dimensions of this spiritual path; for Dr. Rains talks about the impact of Rajneesh's vision on his own work as a therapist.

Palmer's study of the Montreal commune in 1985 was based on qualitative methods: most of the data was gleaned through interviews and attending meetings and social events. The alternative patterns of sexuality and family life are described and the question of the commune's appeal for women is raised. It is postulated that the Rajneesh "experiment" in patterns of work, sexual relationship and sex roles are extreme responses to changes in the nuclear family, and are perceived by Rajneesh women to offer "spiritual solutions" to problems of intimacy, and family life.

The "Letter From Poona, November, 1989" by James S. Gordon describes Osho's last burst of creativity.

Finally, the epilogue to this volume will address the following questions: did the fall of Rajneeshpuram represent a 'prohetic disconfirmation" à la Festinger, and if so, what effect did this experience have on the organization? What is the significance or "relevance" of this NRM for non-seekers and mainstream Americans who are having a hard enough time figuring out their own culture?

1

RAJNEESH AND THE GURU TRADITION IN INDIA

ARVIND SHARMA

Although Rajneesh disdains to call himself a guru, (Rajneesh, 1972:65) it is perhaps not unfair to view him, and perhaps even to place him, within the broad and pluform guru tradition of India (McMullen, 1976), and to see what light this perspective can shed on his life and teachings. This paper attempts to develop such a perspective in three stages, each of which corresponds to the three parts into which it is divided. The guru tradition as it manifests itself in the religious history of India is reviewed in the first part of the paper. In the second part, Rajneesh's responses to these various manifestations are identified. In the final part an attempt is made to locate Rajneesh within this tradition.

I

The guru tradition in India has assumed such diverse forms over the centuries that its encapsulation within a few pages presents major difficulties. The task becomes somewhat less daunting, however, if the discussion is prefaced by a few historical observations. One of these is the recognition that the *emergence* of the institution is connected with the development of the *asrama* system within Hinduism (Kane, 1974:416). This institution, which started showing signs of achieving definition in the age of the Aranyakas (circa 800-600 B.C.), was destined to become one of the distinguishing features of Hinduism. In its classical formulation, it divided a person's passage through life into the four stages of (1) a celibate student (2) a householder (3) a hermit and (4) a renunciant, with ideally twenty-five years allotted to each. Such differentiation into stages required appropriate instruction for each stage and contributed to the development of both secular and spiritual pedagogy (Kane:321).

By the sixth century B.C., however, competing world-views had emerged in India in the form of Jainism and Buddhism, which shared the spiritual dimension of the Hindu world-view as represented by the concepts of rebirth and *moksa*, but rejected the Hindu institutional framework and substituted for it their own. This bifurcation of the spiritual current of ancient Indian religiosity into what are called the *brhmana* and the *sramana* traditions (the former referring to Hinduism and the latter covering Buddhism and Jainism) is another historical fact worth remarking.

The medieval ages supply an additional category with the rise of Sikhism in the fifteenth century (Singh, 1963:41). Its relevance to the current concerns is obvious on account of its direct connection with the institution of guruship. Finally, religious developments in the post-1800 or the modern period of Indian history are also not without significance. On the one hand, this period saw the glorification of the concept of the belief in Masters encouraged by Theosophy; on the other it saw the rise of Hindu leaders such as Mahatma Gandhi (Gandhi, 1948:113-114) and Ramana Maharsi (Osborne, 1971:Chap 4) to eminence, who themselves had no gurus but gained such stature that they came to be virtually regarded as gurus.

The guru tradition in India, therefore, for the sake of clarity, will be examined as it is found within (1) Hinduism; (2) Buddhism; (3) Jainism; (4) Sikhism; (5) Theosophy and (6) the neo-Hinduism of Gandhi and Ramana.

The Guru Tradition in Hinduism

The guru tradition within Hinduism represents a very complex phenomenon. However, given the importance attached by Rajneesh to meditation it seems best to concentrate on the Advaitic philosophical tradition in this respect.

The Upanisads abound in references to the guru and the need for one (*Taittiriya* I.XI.1, *Chandogya* VI.XIV.2; IV.IX.3, etc) but it is the *Mundaka* (1.2.12) which suggests the criteria for determining who should be accepted as a guru. Two requirements are mentioned: (1) he should be *srotriya* or proficient in the Vedas and (2) *brahmanistha*: one who has realized Brahman (Cenkner, 1983:9). The Advaita tradition developed an intellectual and spiritual rather than an emotional approach to the guru (Cenkner:18). The guru evoked devotion to be sure, but on account of his intellectual and spiritual qualities. This movement was strengthened by Sankara whose "most significant contribution to the institution, which constitutes an advance beyond Upanisadic thought" was to "identify teacher and scripture" (Cenkner:34), which the teacher taught. However, on account of its non-dual character, the Advaita tradition in the end dissolved the relationship of *guru* and *sisya* as implying duality; indeed it can even be said that it takes one beyond duality to equality. William Cenkner notes that "sankara's delineation of the spiritual relationship between *guru* and *sisya* that culminates in the equality of the two is one of his important contributions to India's teaching tradition" (1983:57). He goes on to say (1983:57):

> What separates Saskara from other Hindu teachers is that he leads the student beyond the experience and knowledge of the guru. The guru is finally transcended by the experience (*svanubhava*) of the disciple. Personal experience is the norm and source of liberating wisdom; such experience emerges from a relationship deeply formed in knowledge, but it is raised to nondual experience. In his commentary on the *Gita*, the master Vedantin distinguished between knowledge acquired from scripture and the teacher (*jnana*), and knowledge acquired from personal experience (*vijnana*). Although Sankara places personal experience beyond the teacher and scripture in the developmental process, experience and higher wisdom (*vijnana*) come about in the context of a relationship in the order of knowledge (*jnana*). The living relationship is, in this sense, a source of liberating experience and wisdom.

Two other points may be taken into account at this stage. In the tradition it is assumed that the guru is one who has shed the ego and in fact some Upanisads refer to egolessness as specifically required of a guru (Brhadaranyaka 4.3.33). It is also maintained that, should one be forced to choose between a Brahman-knower and a Veda-knower guru, the disciple should prefer the Veda-knower inasmuch as he/she can transmit the tradition; whereas the Brahman-knower, despite his or her experience, will be lacking the language of discourse through which the experience can be transmitted.

The Guru Tradition in Buddhism

The development of the 'master-disciple' relationship in Buddhism, by contrast, followed an opposite course. In the beginning the Buddha was placed on par with the Arhats, but soon Buddha was accorded a place above them all (Malalasekera, 1966:42-43). In a sense it seems the Buddha was apparently always held in some kind of awe. The last words of the Buddha provide an interesting clue here (Rahula, 1959:137):

> Then the Blessed One addressed the bhikkhus: 'It may be, Bhikkhus, that there may be doubt or perplexity in the mind of even one bhikkhu about the Buddha, or the Dhamma, or the Sangha, or the Path, or the Practice. Ask bhikkhus. Do not reproach yourselves afterwards with the thought: "Our Teacher was face to face with us; we could not ask the Blessed One when we were face to face with him".'
> When this was said, the bhikkhus remained silent.
> A second time and a third time too the Blessed One addressed the bhikkhus ... as above.
> The bhikkhus remained silent even for the third time.
> Then the Blessed One addressed them and said: 'It may be, Bhikkhus, that you put no questions out of reverence for your Teacher. Then, Bhikkhus, let friend speak to friend.

These very last words of the Buddha also contain another interesting development. In effect, Buddha made the scripture the guru, anticipating both Prophet Muhammad and Guru Gobind Singh (Rahula, 1959:136).

Then the Blessed One addressed the Venerable Ananda: 'It may be, Ananda, that to some of you the thought may come: "Here are (we have) the Words of the Teacher who is gone; our Teacher we have with us no more." But Ananda, it should not be considered in this light. What I have taught and laid down, Ananda, as Doctrine (*Dhamma*) and Discipline (*Vinaya*), this will be your teacher when I am gone.

In later Buddhism, known as the Mahayana, the distinction between an esoteric and an exoteric transmission also emerged (Watts, 1957:45-46)—a distinction denied in early Buddhism, known as the Theravada (Rahula, 1952:2). This esoteric transmission is a marked feature of what came to be known as Ch'an Buddhism in China and Zen Buddhism in Japan. "The Chinese claim that the school originated in the following way, though the story is not recorded in any known Chinese text or even Pali or Sanskrit. This, however, is in keeping with the claim [of the] Dhyana School whose teachings were handed down orally or by silent understanding between teacher and pupil and not committed to writing" (Ksiang-Kuang, 1960:16). The following account is suggestive in this context: "Sakyamuni Buddha who had been forced to modify his doctrines to suit the capacity of his disciples, once picked up a flower and held it up for the assembly of monks to see. One of them, Mahakasyapa, responded to this gesture with a smile, indicating that he alone understood the profound truth it signified. After this, when the others had retired the Buddha called this disciple to him, and said: "I have here a True Dharma, a wonderful way leading to Nirvana. This is the reality which is not seen, a very subtle form of the Dharma. I now give it to you for safe keeping; guard it well." A Gatha uttered by Buddha in the presence of Mahakasyapa runs as follows:

"The Dharma is ultimately no Dharma;
The Dharma which is no-Dharma, is also a Dharma;
As I now hand this 'no-Dharma' over to thee,
What we call the Dharma, where, after all, is the Dharma?"

Mahakasyapa then uttered a Gatha to match with the above:

> "Pure and immaculate is the nature of all sentient things;
> From the very beginning there is no birth, no death;
> This body, this mind—a phantom creation it is;
> And in phantom transformation there are neither sins nor merits.

From Mahakasyapa, this knowledge was handed to Ananda, and this transmission is traditionally recorded to have taken place in the following manner:

> Ananda asked Mahakasyapa: "What was it that you have received from Buddha besides the robe and the bowl?"
>
> Mahakasyapa called: "O, Ananda."
> "Yes" replied Ananda.
> Thereupon Mahakasyapa said: "Will you take down the flag-pole at the gate?"
>
> On receiving this command, a spiritual illumination came over the mind of Ananda, and the "Seal of Buddha Heart" was handed over by Mahakasyapa to this favorite pupil" (Ksiang-Kuang, 1960:17-18).

The tradition was carried from India to China by Bodhidharma (circa 520 A.D.) and subsequently from China to Japan.

The Guru Tradition in Jainism

Jaina ideas about a guru may also be considered in this connection, specially as Rajneesh's own background is Jaina (Joshi, 1982:9,189-190). One aspect of the Jaina approach consists in its attitude to non-Jaina gurus, which is very critical. In fact accepting them and their teachings is a form of false belief (Jaini, 1979: 153-154):

> ...this is called *guru-mudhata*. India has long abounded in ascetics and spiritual preceptors of all sorts, preaching numerous doctrines and engaging in an incredible diversity of practices. Although most such teachers profess to be free from attachment to the world, their activities are said by the Jainas to belie this claim. Tantric practitioners,

for example, are widely known to engage in sexual activity and in consumption of meat and alcohol, while many so-called gurus emphasize the development of occult powers that are useful only within the context of samsara. But more important than such considerations is the fact that from the Jaina standpoint the practices of non-Jaina mendicants are simply not effective in bringing spiritual progress. The idea that purity can be gained through bathing in a particular river, by ingesting certain drugs, or by similar activities seems simpleminded to one who has reached the fourth gunasthana. Having seen the validity of the Jina's path, he will never again be tempted to take anyone but a Jaina mendicant as his teacher.

The Jaina attitudes towards their own teachers divides somewhat among sectarian lines. "It should be noted that members of the Digambara laity have had far less exposure to bona fide 'ascetic' teachers than have those of the Svetambara. The extreme severity of restraints incumbent upon a Digambara monk, especially as regards clothing, has tended to keep the number of individuals who undertake this path to a select minimum. Hence the teaching function has fallen mainly upon the shoulders of eleventh-pratima laymen—ksullakas, ailakas, and the female *aryikas*; in terms of guru-upasti such preceptors typically receive the same treatment accorded an actual (naked) monk" (Jaini, 1979:208).

Not only the number of teachers but the manner of teaching also shows sectarian variation. "The ritual of teacher veneration shows some sectarian variation. For Digambaras it involves bowing, and beseeching the teacher to utter the formula blessing 'may your righteousness increase'. The layman may also take this opportunity to confess any vrata-infractions of which he is guilty, or perhaps to assume still further restraints. Svetambaras have retained a very ancient and rather more complex procedure. Called vandana (reverent salutation), this ceremony begins when a lay man or woman approaches a mendicant (preferably of the same sex) and greets him or her as *ksamasramana*, ascetic who suffers with equanimity. There follows a ritual exchange in ancient Prakrit, with both individual reciting their parts from memory. The content of this exchange gives a clear picture of the sort of relation obtaining between Jaina monk and layperson:

> I desire to worship you, *ksamasramana*, with very intense concentration. (The guru: so be it.) You will have to spent the whole day, fortunately, little disturbed. (The guru: yes.) You are making spiritual progress. (The guru: yes, and so are you.) You are unperturbed by your sense organs? (The guru: yes.) I ask pardon, ksamasramana, for my daily transgressions. (The guru: I too ask pardon.) I must engage in pratikramana [confession] to you, ksamasramana, for any day-by-day lack of respect...anything done amiss through mind, speech, or body, through anger, pride, deceit, or greed, through false behavior and neglect of the sacred doctrine at any time; whatever offence may have been committed by me, forbearing monk, I confess and reprehend and repent of it and cast aside my past self" (Jaini, 1979:208-209).

The Guru Tradition in Sikhism

The guru tradition within Sikhism may be looked upon as passing through two distinct phases. The first phase is represented by the ten gurus, beginning with guru Nanak (1469-1539). Nanak saw the guru in the following role.

> *The guru.* The Bhaktas and the Sufis had emphasised the necessity of having a spiritual mentor; Nanak went further and made the institution of the guru the pivot of his religious system. Without the guru, said Nanak, there could be no salvation. He was the guide who prevented mankind from straying from the straight and narrow path of truth; he was the captain of the ship which took one across the fearful ocean of life. But the guru, insisted Nanak, was to be regarded as a guide and not a god. He was to be consulted and respected but not worshipped. Nanak accepted for himself the status of a teacher but not a prophet; in his writings he constantly referred to himself as the slave or servant of God (Singh, 1963:41).

The second phase is represented by the declaration of Guru Gobind Singh (1666-1708) that "the line of gurus was to end with him and the Sikhs were thereafter to look upon the *granth* as the symbol of all the ten gurus" (Singh, 1963:95).

It must be borne in mind that according to the Sikh tradition the word guru is "not to be applied to anyone except the ten gurus of the Sikh faith, the Granth Sahib...and for the collective God inspired congregation of the Sikh people...except for these no one else may be called guru" (Talib, 1976:91).

The Guru Tradition in Theosophy

The last quarter of the nineteenth century witnessed the emergence of Theosophy. It was originally incorporated in New York in 1875 but subsequently established its headquarters in Adyar, India. Its commitment to the guru tradition is apparent in at least two ways: (1) in the belief that the Mahatmas of Tibet communicated occult secrets to one of its founders, Madame Blavatsky (Farquhar, 1967:279) and (2) in its belief that a class of Adepts provides spiritual guidance to humanity. Its views on this point are presented below:

> It is foolish for men to wrangle over the question of the superiority of one teacher or one form of teaching to another, for the teacher is always one sent by the Great Brotherhood of Adepts, and in all its important points, in its ethical and moral principles, the teaching has always been the same.
>
> In the earlier stages of the development of humanity, the great Officials of the Hierarchy are provided from outside, from other and more highly evolved parts of the system, but as soon as men can be trained to the necessary level of power and wisdom, these offices are held by them. In order to be fit to hold such an office a man must raise himself to a very high level, and must become what is called an Adept.
>
> A large number of men have attained the Adept level...but always some of them remain within touch of our earth as members of this Hierarchy which has in charge the admin-

istration of the affairs of our world and of the spiritual evolution of our humanity.
This august body is often called the Great White Brotherhood.

A few of these great Adepts, who are thus working for the good of the world, are willing to take as apprentices those who have resolved to devote themselves utterly to the service of mankind; such Adepts are called Masters (Farquhar, 1967:279-280).

The Guru Tradition in Neo-Hinduism

The guru tradition is traceable within neo-Hinduism but with certain limitations. One major figure of neo-Hinduism, Vivekananda (1863-1902), was the disciple of Ramakrishna (1836-1886) (Renou, 1962:228) but interestingly enough Ramakrishna himself was not in any direct line of disciplic succession. He was given spiritual instruction by more than one master (Saradananda, 1952:248), in one case by a woman (1952:248). It is through his connection with Totapuri (1952:246), who coached him in Advaita, that he is brought within the formal nexus of *guru parampara* or the guru-tradition. Mahatma Gandhi did not have a guru and not only did Ramana Maharshi (1879-1950) not have a guru (at least in this life), he did not always use the word guru to refer to a human guru—in the usual understanding of the term. "S.S. Cohen has recorded a conversation on this subject with Dilip Kumar Roy, the celebrated musician of Sri Aurobindashram:

> Dilip: Some people report Maharshi to deny the need of a Guru. Others say the reverse. What does Maharshi say?
>
> B.: I have never said that there is no need for a Guru.
>
> Dilip: Sri Aurobindo often refers to you as having had no Guru.
>
> B.: That depends on what you call Guru. He need not necessarily be in human form. Dattatreya had twenty-four Gurus—the elements, etc. That means that any form in the world was his Guru. Guru is absolutely necessary. The

Upanisads say that none but a Guru can take a man out of the jungle of mental and sense perceptions, so there must be a Guru.

Dilip: I mean a human Guru. The Maharshi didn't have one.

B.: I might have had at some time or other. And didn't I sing hymns to Arunachala? What is a Guru? Guru is God or the Self. First a man prays to God to fulfil his desires, then a times comes when he does not pray for the fulfilment of a desire but for God Himself. So God appears to him in some form or other, human or non-human, to guide him as a Guru in answer to his prayer (Osborne:117-118).

Mahatma Gandhi greatly admired Raychandbhai but after recording his admiration for him, he remarks in his autobiography:

And yet in spite of this regard for him I could not enthrone him in my heart as my Guru. The throne has remained vacant and my search still continues.

I believe in the Hindu theory of Guru and his importance in spiritual realization. I think there is a great deal of truth in the doctrine that true knowledge is impossible without a Guru. An imperfect teacher may be tolerable in mundane matters, but not in spiritual matters. Only a perfect *gnani* deserves to be enthroned as Guru. There must, therefore, be ceaseless striving after perfection. For one gets the Guru that one deserves. Infinite striving after perfection is one's right. It is its own reward. The rest is in the hands of God.

Thus, though I could not place Raychandbhai on the throne of my heart as Guru, we shall see how he was, on many occasions, my guide and helper. Three moderns have left a deep impress on my life, and captivated me: Raychandbhai by his living contract; Tolstoy by his book, *The Kingdom of God is within you* ; and Ruskin by his *Unto this Last*. But of these more in their proper place (Gandhi:113-114).

II

What does Rajneesh have to say about these understandings of the guru tradition?

The Guru Tradition in Hinduism

Rajneesh seems to accept the requirement that the guru should be a *brahmanistha* or established in the knowledge of the ultimate reality. He declares: "Only he is a teacher who has discovered *himself*, who has devised a key *himself*, who has known the source of knowledge *himself*, who has encountered the reality *himself*" [emphases added] (Rajneesh, 1972:203). But what are his views about the guru being a *srotriya* ?

The word *srotriya* can be understood in two senses: in the literal sense of one well-versed in sruti or the Vedas and in the more general sense of one who can communicate the knowledge of reality to a textual community or any community for that matter. For what the Vedas really do is to serve as a cultural vehicle for spiritual communication among the Hindus, in the same way as the Bible does among the Christians, for instance. Rajneesh's concept of the guru transcends both these senses of *srotriya*. The first sense is clearly too restrictive. The second is broader but needs to be universalized even further. Rajneesh maintains that all the religions represent "local keys" and "so I am struggling and devising keys that are, in a way, universal— not for a particular localized culture, but for the human mind as such" (Rajneesh, 1972:209).

The Guru Tradition in Buddhism

Rajneesh clearly favours the idea of an esoteric experiential transmission of the enlightenment-experience as developed within the Zen tradition. He presents his own version of the emergence of the tradition in India (Rajneesh, 1972:204-207) and its transmission to China and then remarks: "That secret cult has flowered now in the exoteric cult of Zen. *Zen Buddhism is just an esoteric Bodhidharma tradition.* Now, whatever Suzuki is talking or others are talking around the world, is from the exoteric knowledge, not from the esoteric one. Now that has become hidden again. It has again disappeared. But the current is there. It continues. That is why there are esoteric circles."

The Guru Tradition in Jainism

In Rajneesh's writings references to the Jaina concept of the guru as conspicuous by their absence, although he hails from a Jaina family (Joshi, 1982:9). There is, however, the following biographical anecdote which may be of interest: "When still a young child, he became very sad over the death of a sister and refused food for a long period of time. One day he encountered a Jain *sadhu* who wore only a loin cloth and took his food in a begging bowl. He liked the simplicity of this *sadhu's* ways so much, he also began to dress like him and began taking food again, but only in a begging bowl. In order to get him to eat, his mother had to arrange it so that the food was given him in the bowl, after he had begged for it" (Rajneesh, 1972:228).

Rajneesh belongs to the Digambara or 'sky-clad' branch of Jainism.This branch of Jainism is distinguished by comparatively more severe rules of asceticism; (Jaini, 1979:39,41) and denial of Arhathood to women (1979:39-40). In these respects Rajneesh has departed from his background or may even have reacted against it. He is not against materialism per se and women enjoy at least an equal if not an even somewhat favourable position in comparison to men in relation to enlightenment. On the other hand, inasmuch as the Digambaras adopt a more "human" position in relation to Mahavira vis-a-vis the Svetambaras, he would connect with the more 'humanitarian' tradition (1979:34).

The Guru Tradition in Sikhism

The guru tradition in Sikhism is epresented by two developments, as indicated earlier. The first of these is the succession of the ten gurus. Rajneesh views this aspect with approval. He suggests that Guru Gobind Singh had to terminate the succession because no one was ready to receive the live transmission (Rajneesh, 1972:144-145). The second development, however, namely, the installation of the Granth as guru, is not consistent with Rajneesh's view that "knowledge can be preserved only by living persons, not by books" (1972:193).

The Guru Tradition in Theosophy

Rajneesh seems favorably disposed towards the idea of esoteric groups, also favoured by Theosophy (1972:185). At the same time, however, he also distinguishes his own enterprise from them.

> I have been in contact with many esoteric groups. I have known many living persons, who are still alive, who belong to some group. I have known many keys which were delivered by authentic teachers. But no key of the old tradition is enough, so I am devising new keys. Because I am devising new keys, I am not directly concerned with any esoteric groups, as each esoteric group is interested in and is entrusted with a particular key to preserve. I am not interested in a particular key. I am interested in devising new methods, new techniques, new keys, because all the old keys have become in many ways irrelevant (1972:208).

The Guru Tradition in Neo-Hinduism

Neo-Hinduism *theoretically* continues to accept the necessity or at least the desirability of having a guru; Rajneesh seems to share this view although he expresses the point in terms of *discipleship* rather than guruhood. Thus he says: "I deny being a guru, but I do not deny your being a disciple...discipleship is something without which nothing is possible" (1972:65).

In one respect, however, there is an important difference. Even though some neo-Hindu leaders such as Vivekananda founded Orders; it is widely accepted in neo-Hinduism that individuals can gain salvation on their own without having to *belong* to an esoteric group. Even when the virtue of *satsanga* or the company of fellow-seekers is extolled, it is not carried to the point of claiming that only through an esoteric group can one achieve salvation. Rajneesh sounds a different note—questioning both the ability of people to make it by themselves without a guru (even in rare cases?) and the ability of people to make it by themselves without banding with fellow-seekers. He declares:

> Awakening is possible even in a single moment.
> In that single moment,
> ONE CAN EXPLODE into the Divine.
> That is possible, but generally it never happens.
> One has to struggle for continuous lives,
> because the problem is arduous and
> **one cannot awaken himself.**
> It is very much like this:
> if one is asleep in the morning,
> there is every possibility
> > that **one can dream he is awake.**
> > though he will not be awake.
>
> A group of persons decide collectively
> to make some effort.
> Then it is more possible that sleep can be broken.
> So **awakening is really A GROUP WORK!**
>
> It can happen individually,
> and each individual is capable of doing it alone.
> > BUT IT NEVER HAPPENS SO!
>
> The actual working is different,
> because we never work to our utmost capacity,
> we never work beyond a ten percent part of the mind.
> Ninety percent remains JUST POTENTIAL.
> It is never used (1972:217).

III

Conclusion

Rajneesh's attitude to Guruship seems to represent an innovative combination of the Zen and Advaita Vedantic traditions in this respect. On the face of it this must sound like a paradox, the kind of paradox he would revel in. But inasmuch as both the traditions only confer an instrumental value on instruction and acknowledge the intrinsic value of religious experience alone, both of them share the orientation which has distinguished Rajneesh's own approach to the issue. To see this convergence let me first cite the quintessential summation of the Zen tradition:

> A special transmission outside the scriptures;
> No dependence upon words and letters;
> Direct pointing to the soul of man;
> Seeing into one's nature and the attainment of Buddhahood (Suzuki, 1949:20).

In the tradition of Advaita its pedagogy ultimately gets swamped by its ontology—by its insistence on the non-duality of reality. The Guru has only a provisional role to play:

> The duality of teacher and pupil is also included in this list of dualities which are not ultimately real. Yes; even these and why, the teaching that is imparted belong to the region of mitthya. The guru, the sisya and the upadesa, all belong to the vyavaharika world which will all be sublated on the dawn of jnana. Even the srutis, the Vedic texts teaching the ultimate truth pertain to the predicament of duality and are annulled in the last resort in the unitary experience of transcendental aloneness. The Vedas too cease to be Vedas in that stage (*yatra veda avedah*) (Sankaranarayanan, 1970:238).

In this sense Rajneesh has appropriated that element in the Guru tradition of India which ultimately points to the dispensability of the Guru. The Guru is like the finger that points to the moon—and is then withdrawn.

2

THE CRAZIES—WHO FOLLOWS RAJNEESH AND WHY

TED MANN

During a bus trip at the Oregon commune I was chatting rather vivaciously with an American sannyasin in his thirties whom I had just met. Passing by sannyasins on the road, our attention became directed to the strange assortment of people there and on the bus. He suddenly turned to me, remarking, "All the misfits from around the world are gathered together here." I had to agree. This sannyasin didn't *appear* to be a misfit, but his work, doing past life regressions, is hardly a conventional occupation. Quite a few others in sight did not appear misfits, but judging from mannerisms, conversation, and some objective evidence, they were loners; outside the commune setting they often would not "fit in."

My research judgement suggested most members of the Oregon commune and the great majority of Rajneesh's followers were socially marginal, i.e. they lived and functioned on the periphery of our society's major institutions. They were not strongly affiliated with established organizations, either professional or occupational, or with unions, traditional religions, political parties, nor with accepted voluntary associations or conventional family groupings. This chapter will clarify, document, and elaborate on these generalizations.

A couple of generalizations from author Sally Belfrage who visited Poona around 1980 and briefly became a sannyasin, expand on the above. She says the Rajneeshees are:

> ...inevitably well-off, if only in the post-hippy flower-child sense of caring little for cash but always able to summon up enough to fly halfway around the world; they have the kind of money 'that seems to breed in its owners dis-satis-

factions requiring extreme measures to put right.' [She adds that] 'through with radical politics, drugs, communal living, feminism, psychoanalysis, encounter groups, they're seeking still more exotic solutions for problems that are luxuries in the first place. Now it's 'who am I?' (Belfrage, 1984:7).

In effect, Belfrage suggests, and the evidence is plentiful, that a majority of Rajneeshees have had a connection with the counter culture, and many with the human potential or growth movement. British sociologist Mullan adds: "I would argue that the 'average' Rajneeshee is middle class, well educated, professionally qualified...divorced at least once, has suffered a 'personal crisis,' has been through mysticism, drugs, politics, feminism and is 'thirtyish'; in short, the counter culturalist brought up to date" (Mullan, 1983:51). Mullan is too facile—there is little evidence that he or she has done more than dabble in mysticism or politics. Indeed, the 13 case studies of sannyasins Mullan provides in his study show that only a minority of these have had all the experiences he lists.

The term counter-culture is a sociological abstraction and open to a variety of definitions. I prefer to conceive of it as a rather amorphous grouping of generally urban, middle class youth sharing a sub-culture with a specific value set. This subculture favours expressive as against instrumental values and leans towards impulse gratification as against its inhibitions; i.e., patterns normally confined to the lower class. Its members devalue or scorn mechanical and non-creative work and, conversely, highly value an expressive outlook that favours lively or ecstatic type experiences typically gained through LSD, dope, sex and/or meditative states. Life is to be experienced not rationalized, feelings are more important than logic and logical analysis. Harvey Cox, the noted theologian, says the members of the counter culture have a "longing for what the consumer culture cannot provide, a community of love and a capacity to experience things deeply" (Cox, 1978:50). The counter culture's social posture is basically rebellious, strongly scornful of established bourgeois work, family and money values. In a lecture, Rajneesh once called his followers "the Crazies"—partly a tongue-in-cheek remark, but it also signified that, from a bourgeois and worldly standpoint, their actions seemed to be crazy: they would work for nothing (for the Master) and make no effort (any longer) to become established or accepted in the "straight" world.

Counter cultural signatures were somewhat more predominant in Poona than in Oregon. At Oregon in September 1982, when I visited the commune, long hair and beards—a trademark of the counter culture—predominated. Most of the women, too, had long hair. Perhaps 10% of the males had short hair and no beard. But when I asked one of these if he didn't feel conspicuous, he replied, "There's been a new ruling by Bhagwan that short hair is now in." Sheela and Arup had short hair, though Rajneesh sported longish hair and a beard. Another objective mark of the counter culture is smoking dope. While not officially approved of, this was common among Rajneeshees, many of whom had smoked dope or tripped acid before becoming sannyasins.

Other eastern religious movements have attracted large numbers of counter culture types. Among these are the 3HO, the Sikh movement, whose followers dress in white, and the Divine Light Mission of Maharaj-ji (Price Maeve, *Sociological Review*, Vol. 27, [2] : 212).

Equally common in the background of Rajneeshees is experience with encounter, primal and Gestalt therapies, the stock in trade of the human potential movement. It is significant that Rajneesh early attracted to Poona leaders or enthusiasts from growth or body therapy centres like Quaesitor in London, England, and Radix in California. The human potential movement participant's interest is in self-realization and self expression. The goal is to achieve an ever greater amount of awareness, creativity, empathy, intuitive insight and the capacity to express one's essence. Of the 13 life stories of Rajneeshees summarized in Mullan's book, 10 had previously investigated one or more human potential therapies. This percentage accords with my observations of the cult's following in four countries.

One noted writer on the human potential movement is John Rowen. He claims that the movement has three main principles:

the salience of an intense and profound group experience in which certain break-throughs and insights occur; "the existential experience of being totally alone and totally responsible for oneself; and the ecstatic peak experience where for a (brief) moment the pattern and unity of everything and everybody...can be glimpsed" (Mullan, 1983:21).

In the Poona ashram, according to interviews, many sannyasins underwent intense group identifications and/or ecstatic experiences. This occurred either in therapy groups or during active meditations like kundalini, or while dancing in the Music Group. Thus, one sannyasin, commenting on the cathartic effects of the dynamic meditation said, "Bhagwan invented a lovely way to wash away your crazies" (*Orange Juice* :6). Another added, "I can let out just about anything... [in the dynamic]. Through it I can make my inner being free of everything" (*Orange Juice* :6). Many full-time ashramites, i.e. those living in the ashram, experienced profound feelings of close identification with the group and with Rajneesh. Such highs functioned to hook sannyasins to the movement, often for years. These ecstasies were seen by many as steps on the way to enlightenment. For growth therapists and habitues of human potential therapies the hazy, mystical notion of enlightenment often functioned as a very powerful carrot. Once enlightened, it was expected that one would live in a state of permanent bliss, or euphoria. Those who had experienced even brief moments of an oceanic merging or other form of mystical fusion were often too easily seduced by hopes of making these states regular and permanent. Wallis has summed it up: "Rajneesh's Tantrism overlapped extensively with the principle ideological elements of the Human Potential Movement, but offered something far more, a path to Enlightenment (Wallis, 1985:6-7).

In the balance of this chapter, we will substantiate the above and elaborate on the kinds of persons who joined the Rajneesh cult. This will be done in part by examining data on the German, American and British movements, the three nations with the largest sannyasin following. A close look at the Canadian sector will buttress the general analysis.

Social Survey Findings

The doctoral thesis by Klaus Peter Horn, mentioned earlier, provides solid survey data on the Poona ashram's population during 1979-80. Two sannyasins who had previously launched social surveys of the ashram for uncompleted postgraduate degrees, donated their data to Peter Horn. He also initiated his own survey. In each case, because the researchers were sannyasins, they received considerable encouragement and cooperation from the ashram's management. Many of the questions asked in the surveys, e.g. "how do you feel about Rajneesh", or "do you want to do more groups", provided useful information to ashram leaders and this helped gain official cooperation. Still, the sceptical may wonder about the reliability of such data. However, my own reception by ashram officials in Poona in 1981, including freedom to explore in depth and unhindered the press office's voluminous clipping files, leads me to believe that many sannyasins and the Poona leaders were quite open to the idea of objective social research and unafraid of what such might reveal. This of course accords with the high degree of professional education which characterized therapists and leaders.

The samples were as follows: 200 German sannyasins, many working in the ashram, questionnaired by Peter-Horn himself and labelled Sample A. (In addition, he completed 20 in-depth interviews with German-born sannyasins.) Secondly, 300 American sannyasins questionnaired by an American psychologist sannyasin and labelled Sample B. Findings from these surveys were printed in the *Rajneesh Newsletter*, June 1, 1981. The third sample, labelled C, was composed of 200 ashram visitors. The fourth embraced 1200 persons, including some ashramites, who attended a morning discourse by Rajneesh, and was labelled D.

The questionnaires to the German sannyasins were first handed out from a booth at the ashram to any interested passers-by throughout a period of several weeks. When this method of distribution seemed too slow, Peter-Horn approached individual sannyasins and sought to gain their cooperation by direct enlistment. This worked better. Sannyasins recruited in these two ways filled out the questionnaire elsewhere and returned it to the booth. Ashram authorities allowed the booth to be set up in a convenient location, but did not publicly try to sell sannyasins on the project.

The data by age delineates the youthful membership of the cult. Thus, 69.7% of the ashram workers fell between 26 and 35 years of age, while 8.3% were younger. Of 200 ashram visitors, 43.5% fell into the 26-34 age category, while 3.3% were 25 or under. Of the 1200 at morning discourse, 48.8% were 26-34 and 23.4% were 25 and under. Of the ashram workers ("ashramites"), only 22% were over 35 years of age. In sum, those living and working in the ashram tended to be older than visitors. This was apparently the same at the Oregon commune: one figure they quoted in 1983 is that the average Rajneeshee worker there was 38 years old.

Ethnic analysis showed some differences both between the visitors and the ashramite population. Among the visitors, the Germans constituted 20%, Americans 16%, British 16%, Australians 7%, Indians 7%, Dutch 6%, Canadians 4.5%, French 4.3%, Italians 4%, Swiss 3%, and Japanese 2%. The remaining 9% included Danish, Swedish, New Zealanders, Irish, Israeli, East Germans, Belgiums, South Africans, Brazilians, Argentineans, Norwegians, Mexicans, Chileans, Greeks, Spanish and Malaysians, in that order. Among the 327 ashramites, the ethnic breakdown favoured the British and Americans, as follows: British 28%, Americans 21%, Indian 13%, Canadian 7%, Australians 6.7%, German 6.7%, Dutch 3.7%, and Italian 2.5%. The rest included a smattering of French, New Zealanders, Swiss, Danes, Germans, Japanese, Iranians, South Americans, Portuguese and Filipinos.

A socio-economic analysis of the German sannyasin sample showed that 56% of their fathers had had a college or a university education. Most of the mothers had been full time housewives. Some 41% of the fathers, according to Peter-Horn, had a working class background. Financially, 62% of the German sannyasin parents earned, in 1979, $1500 monthly, while 38% earned $2000 or more monthly and 7% earned as much as $6000 per month. In the American sample (B) the majority (81%) were of middle class background and described their life as successful: 85% had had some college education and 68% *said* they had completed college. Sixty percent had been sannyasins less than 2 years (Wallis, 1985:7).

Analyzed by sex, in the German sample, 55% were women, while the American sample (B) was 64% female. Ecologically, 70% of the German sannyasins came from big cities, as against 60% of the Americans.

The German sannyasin sample analyzed in terms of length of stay in Poona, found 43% were first timers with the balance being second or third timers. 62% had been there $\frac{1}{3}$ months and wanted to stay six months. Some 31% didn't know how long they wanted to stay. Only 23% had professional obligations that would oblige a definite returning time. The rest theoretically could stay till their money ran out. Some 48% participated in group therapies; 32% worked for the ashram; 4% participated in its university courses; 15% engaged in activities outside the ashram. Of the sample's ashramites, most earned this coveted status upon their third visit to Poona; 16% of them had spent more than 1 year in the ashram.

Of the American (B) sample, 49% worked in the ashram and 60% wanted to stay in Poona indefinitely. When the A and B samples were compared, it emerged that the Germans took longer to decide whether to become a sannyasin and also whether to work in the ashram, i.e. they seemed more cautious.

Of 64 German sannyasin ashram workers, 58 wanted to stay in Poona "forever." Of the 96 Germans (out of 200) who had participated in therapy groups, 50 wanted to stay in Poona forever; the rest were undecided. Of 31 Germans living outside the ashram, 18 or 58% wanted to stay forever and none wanted to go back to Germany. They saw India as a paradise! Of those living outside the ashram, (Sample A), 4% did some trading for money (probably drugs) and a few worked for German companies with an Indian branch, or had businesses of their own (bars, restaurants, theatre groups) or performed services like massage.

Those Germans in Sample A who resided outside the ashram generally felt exploited, especially those living near the ashram. Some paid as much as $400 a month for a one room apartment.

The religion analysis of the German (A) sample showed 38% had a Catholic education, 21% a Protestant upbringing, 39%

claimed no religious education and 1% was of a non-Christian tradition. In the American sample (B), 8% were raised with no specific religious training, 24% were Catholic and 43% were raised in non-Catholic traditions. In Sample D, the figures were 30% Catholic, 27.5% Protestant, 12% Anglican, 9.5% Jewish, 4% Hindu, 1.5% other Indian religions, 5% Islamic and 7% no religious affiliation.

As for connections with the counter culture, 40% of the German sample (A) claimed experience either in cooperatives or communes. Among those with a deep commitment, 75% had experimented with psychogenic drugs. Of the American sample (B), 70% had experienced psychological therapies, mainly methods used in the human potential movement. One third of the German sample had had some experience with spiritual groups which, according to Peter-Horn, was a high percentage (proportionately) for West Germans. Of the American sample, half had lived for some time in California and 50% claimed previous experience with spiritual movements.

Further data from the German (A) sample were revealing. One third liked to be by themselves, but felt they were able to make compromises. A majority had stayed in Poona more than six months and one-third considered their visit as open-ended, having no definite plans to go back. While finding living conditions in India horrible, the majority said the poverty in India affected them less than the inner (spiritual) poverty they had perceived in Germany. Half of them spent their time taking groups which they felt prepared them to progress spiritually. Working in the ashram was considered equally helpful in providing opportunities for inner growth.

A majority said they found themselves gradually lessening their dependence on others while experiencing changes in their social roles and social stereotypes. A majority of respondents from both the A and B samples maintained they had dramatically changed their ways of reacting to crisis situations. Previously, they said, their reactions had been characterized by depression and anger, but now they allowed crises to happen, accepted them and tried to change them into learning situations. Such an attitude may have been acquired by living through the many changes in the cult's ideology and organization. A majority also claimed that after taking sannyas, they had become more clear about their lives and how they wanted to live them. Their goal now was to live in ways conducive to self-realization. Since the German sample was self selected, it may have attracted a disproportionate number with such positive interpretations of their experience.

What was new, they claimed, was living a life of permanent self-confrontation, along with acceptance of the reality of permanent insecurity. They noted no big changes in hobbies or general activities: they claimed the big change was in their subjective approach to reality. Rather than being ruled from outside, now they felt they were more inner directed. Some claimed that after taking sannyas they began having transpersonal experiences. Their perception of external reality expanded, as well as their notions and experience of space. They had developed, too, a belief in reincarnation, in the possibility of enlightenment and in the concept that humans are more than just body, mind and emotions. Later we will examine a sociological study of sannyasins in the Montreal, Canada centre and how they viewed their life changes since joining.

Asked about future plans, 53% of the German (A) sample had no professional plans, and 16% didn't answer the question, suggesting they too were uncertain. The rest, 31%, said they did have concrete professional plans, which Peter-Horn felt constituted a large percentage, since the ideology of the commune was to live totally in the here and now. Of those interviewed in depth by Peter-Horn, the majority were flexible in their approach to the future; having no children or fixed professional obligations and earning a living by short term jobs, they felt independent.

The German sannyasin sample (A) was asked how they viewed their relationship to Rajneesh. According to their answers, either they aimed at self realization or at surrender to Rajneesh. The first category saw their relationship to him as a functional one, i.e. he was seen as a master and as such occupied a specific functional place in their personal development. Within this category, some 18% felt an easy-going or humorous relationship to him. Another 10% saw the relationship as magical, regarding him as a wonder worker. Another 10% percent recognized fear as one component of their relationship. They might say to themselves, "What would happen to me if I drop out?—He would get at me!" Some 5% confessed to feeling resistance or distance from him or an intense anger.

The second category had a devotional relationship to Rajneesh; their attitude was one of trust and surrender. This type, consisting of 44% of Sample A, usually described him in symbolic terms, like "He is the sun or moon", or "He is my life!" or my "one and everything", i.e. they were "in love with him". Peter-Horn described this category as very emotional and anti-rational, whereas the first one, he felt, tended to be reasonably rational, able to accept trans-rational experiences and integrate these into a personal frame of experience. Unfortunately, analysis of these two groups according to their gender was not provided in Horn's thesis.

The British Membership

On the British movement the available data comes from three sources. First, two chapters in Mullan's book published in December, 1983 dealt with the large commune of Medina and includes case studies of 13 sannyasins. Secondly, I subsequently visited, observed and participated in a number of activities at its London Centre. Thirdly, I talked with a few British sannyasins and interviewed four ex-sannyasins.

Medina was the large showpiece commune of England. In December, 1983, it had over 100 adults and 30 children living on 13 acres in a mock Tudor mansion. Mullan emphasizes its counter culture ambience. "Generally one feels back in the 60's, with many bare feet, Jesus sandals and high beard count" (Mullan, 1983:103). But he observed a strong entrepreneurial outlook, typical of many communes. A bit of jargon reminding him of the counter culture was frequent use of the term "Far Out!" In the library, Mullan found books on therapy, educational and humanistic psychology, the new age and the esoteric. The therapy and other program offerings smacked of the human potential movement. "The commune," he wrote, "is heavily into the happiness industry" (Mullan, 1983:111). Its healing centre mainly dispensed orthodox medicine, but also offered courses in holistic health, homeopathy, Shiatsu and regular massage, Tarot reading, hypnotherapy, and a form of acupuncture. All of this emphasizes strong connections with the counter culture and the human growth movement.

Attending its weekend activities, which could attract several hundred non resident sannyasins, he claims most had experimented with some higher education. "The majority were in the professions or the creative arts" (Mullan, 1983:102). He failed to add that a sizeable percentage had failed to complete their courses. In religious background, as noted elsewhere, Catholics and Jews, particularly among the women, stood out. Maritally, "the majority were either divorced or single" (Mullan, 1983:102). Ethnically, the Medina Rajneeshees came from many lands: Austria, Holland, South Africa, Ireland, Denmark, Bolivia and Hungary, besides England. This mixture indicates an interest in travel, and suggests weak ties to home and kin.

Analysis of the 13 sannyasin life stories provided in Mullan's chapter four, reveals that a large majority, ten out of thirteen, had travelled a lot, often through Europe and the far East. These persons were occupationally highly mobile, an important factor making for social marginality. Just over 50% had experimented, previous to taking sannyas, with meditation. All, after 21, were apparently unattached or loosely attached to institutional religion. Of the 13, almost 40% had used dope or LSD. Thirty percent had experimented previously with commune living and the same percentage seemed to have experienced poor or disastrous relationships with their families, especially their fathers. This ties in with their adoption of Rajneesh as a father figure, discussed later in the chapter. About the same percentage had experienced serious mental and/or sexual difficulties.

Other Survey Data

Statistical analysis of the members of the Toronto Centre, in 1982, which claimed around 50 members provides another picture of the movement's followers. In a questionnaire which the Toronto Centre leader filled out, she stated that 24% were under 30, 64% between 30 to 40, and 12% about 40. However observations of those who attended Centre social functions suggested that more than 24% were under 30. Religiously, she said 10—12% were Jewish, 35—40% Protestant and about 30% nondescript. Presumably, the balance, about 23—25% were former Catholics. Other estimates of the number of Jews in the cult were somewhat higher and from other sociological studies of cults, this would not be unexpected. The Centre leader claimed that 60% were college educated, but likely by this she meant they had had some college experience, for a random sampling of the membership gave a figure of only 30%.

Another and useful source of data on sannyasins is provided by two surveys done at Rajneeshpuram by psychologists Latkin, Hagan, Littman and Sundberg of the University of Oregon, in August and October 1983. The first questionnaire seeking mainly demographic data was answered by 732 out of a reported total of 800 resident sannyasins. Of these, 635 fully completed ones were analyzed. In the second survey, 250 sannyasins were randomly chosen from the 635. On open-ended questions, the responses of 100 were utilized. According to defector informants present at the commune at the time of the questionnaire's administration, on certain questions such as marriage state, the answers given were not always truthful, but rather conformed to informal norms. It is also doubtful if the total population at the time was only 800 residents: it may well have been double that figure.

With such reservations, the findings are still of some value. It turned out that the average age was 34, and that 35% came from cities of over half a million. Some 64% claimed they were university graduates, and 36% claimed to have advanced degrees, with 22% owing to degrees in psychology or psychiatry. Three-quarters of those surveyed said they had been sannyasins for over three years. Some 75% also claimed to be married, and among those married, 77% said they were living with their spouses at Rajneeshpuram. (This statistic is especially dubious and reflects "advice given" to sannyasins by Sheela on how to answer the questionnaire.) In the ten years prior to coming to Rajneeshpuram, 97% said they had been successful in their work. Almost half (45%) reported having had four or more jobs in those years. As for work at the commune, the average person had experienced at least one job change, and 16% four or more. In religious affiliation before age 18, 27% reported being Catholic, 30% Protestant and 20% Jewish: 14% had no such affiliation. Gordon, who is a Jew, notes that Jews, who have drifted away from their faith in large numbers, were touched by Rajneesh's commentaries on Hasidic tales and Hasidism. "Hasidism," he explained, "is the core of Judaism, its heart, just as Zen was the core of Buddhism" (Gordon, 1986:49). In political background, 51% of Rajneeshpuram's sannyasins characterized themselves as liberal, and 11% as formerly radical. Gordon remarks that "people like Deeksha, who had been active in the radical political movements of the sixties and early seventies found themselves agreeing with Rajneesh's critiques of politics...even those who still wanted to change society felt the need for an internal change...a detachment that would protect them from the temptations to egoism and hypocrisy that political activity would inevitably bring" (Gordon, 1986:49-50).

Other answers underlined findings reported earlier. For example, 40% said they first became interested in Rajneeshism through contact with a friend, some 30% through a book or tape. Some 72%, when asked what led them to become a sannyasin, said "Bhagwan, his writings, teaching, love for him". About 10% claimed some kind of 'ineffable experience', was part of their conversion (Symposium on Rajneeshpuram, the development and impact of a Utopian society, at meetings of the Western Psychological Association, Los Angeles). Some 60% said that prior to becoming sannyasins they would not have characterized themselves as religious. Among those with a college degree, 27% had specialized in Arts and Humanities, 33% in Social Sciences, 10% in Natural Sciences, and 10% in the professions. In terms of social background, 32% claimed they were from a professional family and 49% from a white collar home (Preliminary Report 9/14/83, mimeo).

Class Affiliation

There is some debate about the class alignment of Rajneeshees. Mullan claims they are middle class. A leading sannyasin spokesperson at the Oregon commune said (*Toronto Globe*, May

11, 1982:14), "Most sannyasins are upper middle class, well educated and wealthy". It is true that a number of the Indian leaders, such as Lakshmi and Sheela Silverman are wealthy and upper middle class and some other Indians living at Poona came from wealthy backgrounds. Quite a few, perhaps 10% of the non-Indians, were upper middle class, including a handful of millionaires. However, judging from varied observations and survey data, a considerable *majority* come from lower to middle middle-class backgrounds and at best have or had modest, not large, incomes. Thus, the questionnaire of Rajneeshpuram sannyasins reported that, some five years before, i.e., 1978, they were earning on an average between $20,000 and $30,000 (op. cit).

In addition, my observations at Poona, at the London, England Centre, and in Toronto and Vancouver Centres suggests that a sizeable percentage of Rajneeshees were rootless drifters or gypsy types, who moved from job to job and place to place, and seemed unable to settle down long in one place. Thus, for example, one Toronto sannyasin admitted, "I never really had a clear sense of direction. I would move around frequently, when finances dried up, and take whatever job opportunities arose". Again an interview with the head of the Toronto Centre in April 1983 revealed that it had an annual turnover of almost 100% in those living in the Centre. "We're always having to adjust to a new bunch," she added, underlining the restless character of its resident membership. Many of these were younger, probably below 30 years of age.

In another category are the fairly-to-quite successful persons discontented with the fruits of the "rat race". This group included many like Devaraj, Rajneesh's personal physician and the author of a pro-Rajneesh book, who expressed a strong distaste with careerism and from time to time took a holiday from medical practice. These are well established middle class persons, but had a restless seeker predilection and wanted more meaning and fun out of life. Some of these persons may not have been heavily involved in growth groups prior to taking sannyas, but others were.

Various students of Rajneeshism including Mullan emphasize the number of professionals in the membership. My observations and interviews indicate this comment needs elaboration. First, it is the lower status and newer professions that are more common among Rajneeshees:— nurses, masseurs, social workers, teachers, therapists, actors, dancers and the like. This is clarified by an analysis of the occupations of some 39 disciples who received initiation into sannyas, or were spoken to at a darshan by Rajneesh in May 1977—as reported in a volume of his transcribed darshan talks. In this somewhat random sample, 4 were students, 15 were from new or semi-professions like Alexander therapist, cameraman, record producer and Go-Go dancer, and 6 were people from arts and crafts like sculptor, writer or painter. Fourteen or 36% were from accepted professions like architect or dentist. Wallis observes that what is important is that sannyasins were "overwhelmingly (in) occupations either of a creative kind or in which their main role is service to others, particularly of a human developmental kind. What are absent from these lists are occupations...in which the main tasks are routine and highly bureaucratic...former business people, accountants and civil servants...are a minority and do not by any means set the tone" (Wallis, 1985:9). Wallis amplifies this important point, confirmed by my researches, noting that "the typical follower chose specifically not to be located in the industrial, commercial or bureaucratic core of the modern world. Rajneeshees, by and large, and *before* they had become sannyasins, had already rejected the routine predictability of corporate life, its impersonality and rationalization, to pursue a course more concerned with creativity and the imagination, with human contact and with more spiritual values. Those drawn to Rajneesh...had identified themselves with the pursuit of the *expressive* life. Although many...were materially comfortable...this did not constitute their primary definition of the ideal human condition...it was precisely this group...who could concentrate their attention upon the pursuit of the ideal self" (Wallis,1985:10).

Wallis adds, "although what constituted the ideal self may have differed greatly in detail between particular individuals, it contained certain clearly common themes: freedom from the constraint of (fixed) social roles... (or) delaying gratification to achieve knowledge or abilities required in later skilled occupations: ... greater expressivity in themselves and those with whom they interacted: openness, spontaneity and intimacy... (unrestricted)... by role-playing and social conventions; and enthusiasm and joy in life, less burdened by inhibitions... rejection or failure.... Those who had been less successful occupationally or educationally, or who had eschewed the prerequisites of such success, sought recognition of their intrinsic, inner worth, unmediated by universalistic assessment of their worldly accomplishments" (Wallis, 1985).

It is also significant, as Wallis notes, that those drawn to Rajneesh came basically from occupations which could provide them with the time to take off for a trip to India or to Oregon. Hence they were free to travel from their job for weeks at a time. Students, the self-employed or those in senior positions whose employers would accede to requests for special holiday trips, or teachers with long holiday periods were numerous in Poona or found frequently at the Oregon commune. Wallis correctly sums up the type drawn to Rajneeshism by noting that "the attitude and orientation (of these people) was not one that would readily have accommodated to the regulation, materialism, instrumentalism, emotional repression and restricted openness and sincerity required for successful accomplishment" in bureaucratic jobs (Wallis, 1985:11).

Seekers—The Process of Seeking

Sociological experts on the cults describe the most common type of follower as the spiritual seeker. These are numerous among Rajneeshees. Gordon notes, speaking of the sannyasins at Poona, "most of them have the edgy discomfort of the seeker, the itch of the rebellious and unfulfilled, the apprehensive self-absorption of the narcissistic" (Gordon, 1986:47). In interviews some describe themselves in precisely these terms. Thus, one sannyasin told me, "I am a seeker: I am always looking for new experiences and relationships." Another sannyasin said, "I was following the spiritual scent, but (previously) something was lacking". A third emphasized: "I was searching for something to fulfil me... I never did find it, so I was going on, moving, searching, from one city to another, but not really knowing what it was".

Specifically Rajneeshees may be classified as mostly freshman seekers. This means they are under 40, are seeking with great eagerness and are often willing to make a strong commitment. The contrary sociological type, veteran seekers, are typically over 40, predominantly women and tend to flit, without settling down, from one unconventional religious group to another. Rajneesh's sannyasins have made a commitment, though a considerable percentage did leave within a year or two. A good many who did leave were still seeking. Gordon (1986) describes two of these and I met others. Many, as noted earlier, had previously belonged to other religious or para-religious groups and, after being disillusioned, moved into Rajneeshism. For example, a number were attached to Transcendental Meditation, a few having even risen to trainer status therein.

There appears to be a definable pattern in this process of drifting from one movement to another. It has been uncovered by Professor Metta Spencer, sociologist at the University of Toronto, and described in a paper (unpublished) she gave in 1982 at a conference entitled, Sub-cultures of Psychotherapy. Studying a large number of therapists and their patients in the Metro Toronto area, she discovered that when clients shifted from one therapist to another, usually because he/she was not meeting their expectations, they frequently shifted to someone a bit more unconventional or unorthodox. From her data, she constructed a continuum of therapists and patients, extending from psychiatry and conventional psycho-analysis on the right end, to the more unorthodox on the left; i.e. Primal, neo-Reichian, and on the far left, therapies based on past life exploration. The pattern she observed in studying scores of respondents was that both clients and therapists, when dissatisfied, typically shifted one or two degrees or "steps" from right to left on this continuum. In short, they chose an approach just a little more unconventional or unorthodox but seldom made a big leap from an orthodox to a quite unorthodox far left therapy.

Preliminary work by Professor Spencer now suggests the

same principle holds for persons leaving new religious movements. When these shift allegiance, they tend to change to a group a little more unusual or unorthodox than the one previous. This is exemplified by sannyasins doing TM. Typically, they may have gone from TM to a Yoga group or to someone like Swami Muktananda and then on later to Rajneesh. In India and elsewhere, some spiritual seekers left Theosophy to follow Rajneesh. Other Rajneeshees I have met have been in one form or another of Reichian or neo-Reichian therapy—either as clients or therapists—and then switched to Rajneesh. A study of the Toronto Rajneesh Centre noted that its members had previously been involved in massage, yoga, primal therapy, or Arica, a group led by a South American guru figure named Oscar Ichazo. Sociologists have attempted to develop various categories of seekers and hangers-on of new religious movements. One of the most interesting of such attempts is found in Professor William Bainbridge's book, "Satan's Power", which analyzes the Process Church. First, Bainbridge lists three similar groupings: the social rejects of the counter-culture which he called problematic riffraff; exploiters who hang around religious centres looking for free food and hand-outs; and "religious bums", i.e. confirmed drifters who feed on a movement psychically. Observations of the Toronto centre in 1982 indicated it had none of these types. A "bum" would most likely be "centred out" and made to feel unwelcome. For instance, a college student in one of my classes who visited the Centre in scruffy working class attire was quickly made to feel unwelcome and left. The exploiters would also find it unappealing because nothing was offered for free; even the simplest meditation cost $2.

However, Bainbridge describes three other types of seekers, conventional hangers-on, veteran and freshmen seekers and these were represented in the Toronto Centre. The hangers-on were those not fully convinced or converted, yet willing to go along with most of the group's activities. They were still "shopping". The leader at the Toronto Centre acknowledged their presence and said that about 50% of this type finally joined. Among the freshmen seekers were young females (around 21 years) with, to quote a student researcher, "attractive faces and nice bodies". Many of these were affectionate with male sannyasins at the Centre and on the whole appeared quite caught-up, if not overwhelmed, with the free love, fast-moving pace of the group. A few sannyasins around 35 or older, who had shopped around a lot in spiritual groups and could be regarded as veteran seekers, were also in the Toronto group.

As in other typologies, overlapping occurs, as individual sannyasins may fit two or occasionally three categories. This does not invalidate the typology, for it does throw some light on the considerable variety of seekers within Rajneeshism. Gordon has commented on the wide variety of persons drawn to Rajneesh. He writes that sannyasins "in spite of their similar orange dress and their malas...are very much individuals and individualists" (Gordon, 1986:45). Specified sannyasins were aware of this variety in the membership and had ways of expressing it. For example, Mullan mentions one as saying, "some of the best people he had met were Rajneeshees, while other Rajneeshees were the worst creeps he had ever met" (Mullan, 1983:105). In my interviews or conversations I encountered similar comments from members or ex-sannyasins.

The Appeal

The appeal of Rajneeshism may be analyzed in several different ways. On the one hand, a certain specific experience such as the dynamic meditation seems to draw individuals into the cult. Such individual items have been described by sociologists Bromley and Shupe as 'hooks'. On the other hand, there is the total or overall appeal of the large communes like Poona, Oregon or Medina, which caters to a wide spectrum of human growth or "happiness industry" interests.

The draw of the large commune stems first from its provision of something for everyone. It is the same marketing principle that animates the modern service university, which offers courses on just about anything; or the American big city drugstore that sells not just drugs, but groceries, shoes, tobacco, candles; in fact, almost everything the public wants. Rajneeshism latched onto this principle in the late 70's. In essence, it meant offering any and all kinds of activities, therapeutic, educational, mystical, sexual, that promised to meet a consistent, reliable consumer demand. So by 1977-78, Poona offered over a dozen therapies, various meditations, music and dancing, daily arts and crafts, so-called university courses and seminars, a variety of massages, the isolation or tranquillity tank, etc., etc. Here for almost the first time was available a broad range of the conventional growth therapies along with the promise of ecstatic or mystical experiences and the possible attainment of the ultimate in self-realization, i.e. enlightenment. The offerings expanded up to 1981.

Originally Rajneesh's teaching was geared to egocentric or narcissistic individuals, with some acquaintance with growth groups, and a declining interest in socio-political change. Their hope was in their own self-improvement, or reduced stress and inner conflict. Politics was out. Rajneesh's program was an eclectic mix calculated to appeal to those many westerners unattached to one given psychotherapeutic system, while looking for variety and novelty in growth therapies. And the promise of enlightenment was likely to attract especially those followers of the human potential movement intrigued by transpersonal psychology or the burgeoning American West Coast interest in mysticism or New Age concepts.

This smorgasbord of offerings was widened by 1983 in Oregon to include half a dozen holistic health offerings— including how to slip down or drop smoking—to include dehypnotherapy, plus a variety of strictly physical enjoyments from horseback and aircraft rides, boating and swimming, to river rafting. To complete the Club Med appeal, discos, bar lounges and gaming tables were made available in late 1983. There were few restrictions on having a good time. This mix appealed to those in the under 40 generation who ascribed to a qualified or thoroughgoing hedonistic outlook, including those hooked onto travel to exotic places and experimenting with novel ideas or groups. Accommodations with good vegetarian meals at $40 a day made all this especially attractive to the low budget seeker or traveller. To complete this broad appeal was a friendly, easy-going, experimental and relaxed ambience, clean and tidy surroundings and a highly efficient provision of the various services. And there was no pressure to tackle groups or other activities according to an imposed system—each could try out the offerings according to his or her taste and inclinations. Hence the customer reigned supreme.

In one of the Tantra books, Rajneesh advocated "being loose and doing what comes naturally". Thus, his path is made to sound supremely easy. One sannyasin in an article in their magazine called *Orange Juice* says "You need not obey the Master. You just have to be around, available, that's all. His presence is enough to create the seduction" (*Orange Juice*, 1982:7). The result was that once enjoying this almost idyllic way of life, the non-sannyasin or the newly initiated Rajneeshee would likely want to stay indefinitely. This observation is confirmed by the high percentage of sannyasins and visitors, noted in the survey data, who expressed an interest in staying in Poona indefinitely. The fact is getting initiated was easy, there were no tough moral demands on sannyasins and no daily discipline. And one got a new name, a new identity. Living at Poona, too, was a hot-house or protected cocoon type existence. Stresses were almost non-existent. One sannyasin describes this in *Orange Juice* as follows:"In Poona I immersed myself in the ego-smashing therapies, danced until I'd drop in music group and simply enjoyed loitering about in his beautifully intense Buddhafield. 'Oh bliss,' I thought, 'this is what life is all about'.... The challenge really begins, when I am divorced from this loving support and out in the 'real world'" (*Orange Juice*, 1982:5). There is evidence that when some sannyasins left the Poona ashram for the "real" world, they began to falter and within a year or two had effectively quit the movement.

The message seemed to be do what comes easy for you, do what comes naturally and let it all hang out. Sannyasins into dope or easy sex or whatever were allowed to maintain their lifestyle. Male disciples were given the honorific title of Swami. The women were called Ma, which symbolized mother, but had none of the heavy or tiresome duties of being a real mother. Both genders could easily feel part of a special and avant garde community. These aspects would appeal to drifters, the deviant, the undisciplined, the creative, etc.

In another sense the emphasis on group experience and self realization meant Rajneesh meditation centre or commune life resembled a dream factory or utopia. Anything now seemed possible. Moreover, one could, without serious criticism, come and go from the Poona ashram or from the participation in any given Rajneesh Centre. The German sample in Peter-Horn's study described earlier evidences of this pattern.

Specific experiences may hook individual seekers. Those accustomed to reading books on spiritual states or groups could get hooked by reading one or more of Rajneesh's books, or parts of his books reprinted in ashram periodicals like the *Rajneesh Newsletter* or *Sannyas*. One sannyasin told me, "I read a book of his and bam it hit me. I knew he was for me". Another said, "It was a book, the *Psychology of the Esoteric*. I read between the lines and it was immediate recognition". In his study Gordon has confirmed that some were drawn in by reading Rajneesh saying things which confirmed "fleeting thoughts, perceptions or feelings that they had suppressed" (Gordon, 1986:49).

The sexually repressed or hungry could get hooked and/or kept in the movement by the easy accessibility of sex without guilt. All around in the communes were eager and attractive partners. One could change partners quickly with no group sanctions. Also those longing for ecstatic or intense experiences as a way of validating a change of lifestyle, were hooked by cathartic experiences while doing a kundalini, or a dynamic meditation. Once hooked, they probably soon sought other more intense experiences. It is instructive that wherever I've visited Rajneesh Centres, in Europe or North America, the majority of participants were non-sannyasins. Sannyasins had gone through that type of experience and were interested in something else.

Participants in growth therapies do get hooked into taking more groups. This is a well known phenomenon in the human potential movement. In certain groups they experience a sense of greater inner freedom, or personal power, or energy and they return, looking for more. After ten or twelve, however, the experience begins to wear thin.

Another draw is that Rajneesh was pictured in ashram magazines and by sannyasins as someone who can create the changes anyone needs or wants. He is portrayed as a benevolent-looking ever-smiling Santa Claus figure who will see to it that you enjoy life more, live in the now and eventually even become enlightened. The seeker just needs to be in his presence and soak in his energies. In Oregon, that's what the seeker got, because having moved into "silence", sannyasins didn't hear him speak for years. For many, his early success in drawing huge crowds and his appealing prose in numerous books and his photographs validated him as a Master. It helped that he made few explicit demands, he exuded goodwill, he proclaimed his love for you and all sannyasins. All seemed to be happy—they were always pictured smiling. In sum, quite a few visitors at Poona too were attracted by the quality of his followers. Gordon quotes one sannyasin, whom I'm confident spoke for many when he said "those at Poona seemed freer, happier, than any collection of people I had ever seen" (Gordon, 1986:54).

It is important as well that for the intellectually rebellious, whether it be political or religious, Rajneesh's ideas made a strong appeal. They called for a radical transformation of society and their revolutionary sweep was calculated to draw in avant garde types or advanced intellectuals who felt strongly about society's evils. Rajneesh repeated anti-authoritarian themes that counter-cultural types or the political radicals felt strongly about and he said it all with such poetic style and distinction that he touched the hearts of many in these categories.

While the allegiance of many seekers to Rajneesh can be explained by these hooks, another powerful draw was the large commune with its utopian and emotionally nourishing ambience. Something of this has already been noted. Several of the large communes in Germany, e.g. Berlin and Cologne, apparently exhibited a similar attractive power. The fact that Sheela decided in 1984 to close down smaller European centres while encouraging centralization in half a dozen of the larger ones may be, in part, attributed to the cult's realization that the large commune had special appeals, and was functional.

Fundamentally, the large commune, certainly at Poona and Oregon, provided a form of milieu therapy, not possible in the smaller ones. Participants lived in a multi-service community with numerous built-in therapeutic features that furnished a relaxed, tension-dampening, easy-going ambience akin to that of a Roman Catholic retreat centre. Visitors quickly felt far removed from the hurly burly, the jangly noise, tension and competitiveness of the standard American or Western city. Time pressures too were minimal. While there were line-ups, those waiting had plenty to talk about and displayed few signs of tension or impatience. Children were few in number and rarely made noisy demands; nor did they seem unhappy or unruly. Almost everyone in these communes was relatively young, wore the same garb and seemed in a friendly, holiday mood. It was like being on a holiday with an affectionate family group. Sex was readily available. Nudity was common in co-ed showers and certain therapy groups which helped to create the atmosphere of the liberal bourgeois home. This was doubtless experienced as nourishing or therapeutic by the stressed out or neurotic. Finally, in both Poona and Oregon there was sufficient structure in the daily routine, as well as the communal status system, to convey a sense of genuine security. The many steps taken to protect the life of Rajneesh, the corner-stone of the commune, helped maintain this sense of security. This family would last, was the constant message.

It was the success of Poona, Oregon and Medina in drawing crowds, providing recruits for sannyas initiation and in earning money that gave the cult its power and wealth. However the relaxed therapeutic ambience as well as the cafeteria-style daily program at the communes catered to the kind of people drawn to Rajneesh. On the one hand, they fostered a social situation favouring both self-expression and a sense of inner freedom. For while there were some regular structured events, e.g. the morning discourse at Poona, or the drive-by's at Oregon, the visitor was given many appealing options and no sense of pressure or obligation to continue any given group or activity. Besides, the very brevity of the therapy groups (4 days at Poona) permitted constant change in focus or interest. The restless or uncertain could try out this or that, take in a meditation or a dance group for an hour and yet feel no obligation to complete the activity or program. Such a relaxed system accommodated the outlook of counter culture types or drifters. And the absence of rigid rules and times facilitated a holiday ambience. In sum, the commune's daily program was calculated to fit the needs of those who shared an expressive or undisciplined value system. Again, the great variety of available therapies and courses provided those dedicated to self improvement with a cafeteria-style situation. The idea of trying out whatever appealed, limited only by the decision making power of Arup and the group's enrolment, and going along with whatever "worked" made it easy to move from one interesting experience to another. Individual choice generally reigned. Individualistic experimentation was generally encouraged and also helped by the low fee structure. At the same time, daily life at Poona or Oregon was nourishing to egos, fragile or otherwise. Cafeteria-style meals served expeditiously, though strictly vegetarian, were extremely palatable and cheap. At Oregon, too, the quantity was ample and one could go back for seconds and thirds, with no extra charge, as if one were at home. Both communes provided, as well, lots of physical affection; in fact hugging and kissing were virtually institutionalized. Thus, it was easy to feel an integral part of it all.

Transference

A variety of observers at Poona, including a middle ranking German judge who had made a study of the movement in his homeland, emphasized Rajneesh's role and appeal as a father figure. There is evidence that many if not a majority of sannyasins did not get along well with their father or with both parents. This was supported by the results of numerous interviews. Ex-sannyasin Anna Forbes, quoted frequently by Gordon, has told me that she has yet to meet a sannyasin or ex-sannyasin who got along well with his/her parents. Thus, it is reasonable to assume that some of these sannyasins, lacking the emotional security provided by a loving parental relationship, might unconsciously gravitate to an authority figure on whom to lean and to whom to surrender their autonomy. Such a figure must, of course, be prepared to take responsibility for their lives. Rajneesh filled this need. He talked with great authority, claimed enlightenment, was an eminently successful and mature person and presented himself as wise, benevolent and trustworthy. His writings and communes presented a clear life style, with an answer to every question. The many glamorized photographs of him in each commune conveyed a sense of his immediate presence, spiritual power and ready availability for those who needed or wanted such an authority figure. Cult literature, too, encouraged sannyasins to ask for answers to personal questions from Rajneesh by talking to him in their heads as if praying to a deity. In addition, in Oregon, the fuss attending his daily drive-by in a Rolls cast him in the style of an Emperor bestowing loving care on all his subjects. As long as he made this daily drive-by, the impression was left that nothing really can go wrong with the commune and its members.

One intelligent sannyasin interviewed many times, as he slowly moved away from the cult, might epitomize this father figure appeal aspect or element within the membership. He had many unresolved conflicts with his father and admitted to me he went to Poona to find a Daddy and to be told how to be enlightened. On his return to Canada, he began to get attached to another father figure, a professor and supervisor of his Ph.D. program, and gradually wore less and less of the orange. Then, discarding his mala, he left off attending the local Rajneesh group completely. In a year or so he made a successful transition to this new father figure. Our ex-sannyasin now took an objective approach to Rajneeshism. (Later, this professor began playing a distinct Eastern guru role, in both hair style, garb and behaviour.

From a psycho-analytical standpoint, it is possible to explain many sannyasins' devotion to Rajneesh as a case of idealized oedipal transference. Heinz Kohut in his *The Analysis of the Self*, explains the process as follows: basically, the child idealizes the parent as object and then later may transfer this to parental images, which are cathected to the object libido. "Clinical experience demonstrates that a severe disappointment in the idealized oedipal object...may lead to a renewed... search for an external object of perfection" (Kohut:45). "If the genesis of the disturbance relates to the oedipal period...then the idealization of the superego will be incomplete with the result that the person (though he may possess his own values and standards), will forever search for external ideal figures from whom he wants to obtain the approval and leadership which his insufficiently idealized superego cannot provide" (Kohut:49). "In the above cases, there is an 'overestimation' of the love object and it is closely akin to the state of being in love. Such persons are forever attempting to achieve a union with the idealized object since...their narcissistic equilibrium is safeguarded only through the interest and the responses of approval of present-day replicas of the traumatically lost self-object" (Kohut:55). Kohut notes that when this transference happens during a psychoanalysis, there occurs "the projection of the idealized superego unto the analyst" (Kohut:75), and the object, the analyst, is accorded attributes of wisdom and power. He adds: "The patient may attribute grandiose powers to the analyst" (Kohut:83). In our situation, it became clear that when someone makes a similar transference to a guru, such as Rajneesh, he could conceptualize the guru as divine or enlightened, endowed with vast powers and wisdom. Especially if many of those he meets already are "in love" with the guru and consider him enlightened, divine, etc. We will never know the extent to which such a transference phenomenon occurred with Rajneesh but, especially with some women followers, it was present. Gordon notes that a spiritual master is an object of transference (Kohut:36). He admits that "I can see that there are aspects of transference, the transfer of my own childlike dependency and love, my need for a protective and powerful person to Rajneesh and his group leaders" (Kohut:77) without discussing its ramifications. Doubtless this insight helps us understand the following of many of the guru figures.

Another group of followers became hooked on the intense emotional experience felt at Rajneesh communes. They were excited deeply by the lack of sexual restrictions, the frequent hugging and kissing, and the highs experienced in dancing groups or meditations. The commune also met their needs for fun and learning new skills, for creative and artistic self expression and a sense of importance. Something new was always breaking forth, they never got bored. Also, in the commune's intimate family type situation one felt fully accepted. One fortyish highly qualified physical scientist who had observed the cult at arms length for 1 1/2 years, admitted after his second visit to Rajneeshpuram, "First I fell for his books, then I found myself falling *in love with the disciples*. The leader in our group gave so much of himself, I felt Bhagwan was coming through him." He was now very close to joining, as he sampled and got hooked, on the *emotional intensity* of interpersonal interactions. Though not a stranger to growth groups, the freedom and deep feelings of contact at Rajneeshpuram amazed him.

Once attached to a religious movement, it usually takes other kinds of experience to hold a new follower's loyalty. Some Rajneeshees found their devotion maintained by the frequent expressions of affection between sannyasins around the ashram and by the way feelings of love, comradeship or sexual attraction spontaneously flowed back and forth. The commune life often produced a strong family feeling and thus fostered a powerful sense of security. For the neurotic, lonely, fearful or alienated and, specifically, those needing physical expressions of affection, such spontaneous expressions of concern and love were both reassuring and intensely gratifying.

Concrete personal gains made by sannyasins helped keep some in the cult. A questionnaire administered to a random sample of Toronto sannyasins in 1982 included a question on what benefits they had gained from membership. The consensus was that they had gained a more acute awareness of life, were more centred and that their attitudes and emotions were more intense and crystallized. In short, they felt they had apparently become more vital and integrated. If sufficiently evident, these gains would help consolidate loyalties.

The following quotation from Frances Vaughan, an expert on transpersonal psychology and a student of spiritual movements, puts some of our discussion within a broader context. It comes from her article, *A Question of Balance, Health and Pathology in New Religious Movements*:

> From a psychological perspective, motivation for joining spiritual groups may span a broad spectrum of needs. For example, individuals may join a paternalistic group because they are unable to support themselves adequately;

because they feel lonely and isolated and welcome the sense of belonging to a community; because they are looking for a teacher or substitute parent figure to mitigate the awesome uncertainties of existence; because they are personally attracted to the leader or someone else in the group; because they feel empowered to be more effective in the world as a result of group support; because they genuinely want to make a contribution to the well-being of others; because they want to improve social conditions and relieve suffering; because they feel they are actualizing their potential and progressing along a path of spiritual development; or because of a desire to become spiritually enlightened and attain personal liberation from the conflicts of life" (Vaughan, 1982:23).

3

THE WORK OF OSHO RAJNEESH: A THEMATIC OVERVIEW

Swami Anand Jina (Dr. Robert Gussner)

First a word about the title of this paper. To speak of a "thematic approach" unfortunately implies to many that a static list of rationally ordered concerns might capture and contain the vision and work of Osho Rajneesh. "Theme" is usually a part of hopelessly rational discourse. I wish, however, to induct the word into a different, dynamic context.

This context might be suggested by the imagery in the phrase, "the sound of running water", which points to the uniqueness and primacy of each instant. Although a stream runs generally toward the ocean, and thus has a certain apparently "rational" consistency, it changes direction, sound, current and depth in response to the play of terrain and obstacle. Its face changes with the caress of tributaries, rainfall, riverbed, boulders, dams and the melting of primeval snows. The flowing liveliness of existence knows no static, logical oppositions. Rather it moves in the interplay of complementary polarities within some encircling mystery. The Rajneesh movement, likewise, is necessarily a part of this interplay of polarity, a changing element in the interdependent web of existence.

If a succession of themes can be teased out of the Rajneesh movement, they stem more from Osho's spontaneous and comprehensive response to structures of modernity that delay human enlightenment than from any consistent ideology in the usual Western sense. Themes appear because of Osho's desire to share the beauty and vastness of "what he has seen". As a consequence of this desire he has confronted all or most of the 20th century forces that prevent the flowering of human consciousness.

Different themes simply reflect different forces he has fought. They emerged naturally along the shifting lines of this "flightless fight". These forces, as we shall see, root in the whole religious and political past of humanity, "which has not been a blessing, but a calamity". While there is a definite chronological order to the unfolding of themes in the history of the Rajneesh movement, most emphases have been present from the first. A few were new, but most have only rotated to the spotlight at certain times in response to events. Let us recount, then, the principal themes that address modern obstacles to *nirvana*.

1. *Active Meditations*. 1966-68. The first meditation camps addressed the problem of the uniquely repressed, volcanic, modern mind. This tense mind is probably the result of the relentless rationalization of all areas of life in recent centuries. Performance pressures, pace and social "compacting" have all increased. The modern psyche is the result of what Foucault might call state-sponsored "technologies of the self", new types of discourse deployed to subtly manufacture persons from within. It was no good, Rajneesh said, trying to quiet this modern mind by silent sitting. "An unstill mind primarily needs to be exploded, anarchic". One should be total in playfully letting out hurts and emotions. After active release, one can reach a natural silence. Then one can be total in observing the silent mind. The master theme of this movement, as of others, is *awareness*—witnessing thoughts and feelings, being disidentified, able to see them—when you are talking to know that you are talking. "Present centredness" is the alpha and the omega of Rajneesh sannyas: "seeing". The "manifesto document" of this phase of the movement is probably *Meditation: A New Dimension*. The emphasis on dynamic meditation has persisted throughout. It was a time of learning our conditioning—inner social inhibitions, censoring, cancelling, blocks.

2. *Sexual freedom*. 1968-69. The famous Bombay talks blamed anti-pleasure theologies for cutting the root of human love. They created a dead and joyless world. Religions that oppose the higher to the lower, the spiritual and material life, divide man's inner energies. The main religious pattern has been life-and-world-negating. It creates a mind/body split. Its inner civil war

prevents spiritual evolution. It side-tracks humanity into a swamp of vices, guilt and priestly dominance, into exoteric religion. The manifestos here are *From Sex to Superconsciousness* and *Roots and Wings*. Although all his students were still Indian, the controversy that followed marked the end of Bhagwan's hope for any popular work in India. To learn: passionate energy is not our enemy.

3. *Neo-Sannyas*. 1970-73. This new type of sannyas was open to all, including Westerners, without qualifying virtues or traditional vows. It was not renunciation of home, sex and money, but renunciation of pretence and artificiality. It was being natural and personal, based on your present experience—coming from the heart, not head. Going from the unreal to the Real needed a middle stage of being socially real. Besides this, neo-sannyas involved taking a new name, wearing sunrise colours and a *mala*, and having an hour of meditation a day. The orange revolution was, in part, an outrageous rejoinder to angry India, an attempt to simply drown the old sannyas and make Indian sadhus invisible in a sea of Western disciples. Yet it was still Hindu: through love, beyond love. The main literature in this period was the ten volume commentary on the *Yoga Sutras* of Patanjali and *The Book of the Secrets*, a five volume commentary on 112 meditation aphorisms in the *Vijnana Bhairava Tantra*. Discourses from this time taught Westerners to treasure texts of India.

4. *"The Great Experiment" Via Poona Ashram Growth and Therapy Groups*. 1974-77. The "great experiment" plan unveiled a whole new sociology. Its central themes were relating not relationship, commune as family, a new educational pattern, and an identity of the spiritual seeker over against all narrow national, religious or leftist identities. Growth groups multiplied to supplement meditation for catharsis of anger, fear, sadness, wounds. They also modeled the new atmosphere of individual freedom and responsibility. In an historic development, new age therapies and body work were combined with meditation. Groups became a new "preparatory path" for meditation. Bhagwan studied differing types of seekers to find a science of multiple paths. The cultural era of one type of path

for one type of person created by one isolated culture was over. Cultural mixing produced mixed mental types, who needed new types of meditation.

The main thrust of this period was to create members fit and able to live with other people in the new social pattern. The frontispiece quotation of *The Sound of Running Water* sums up the central theme of this period with the Words of Gurdjieff, quoted in Ouspensky:

> Do not think that we can begin straight away by forming a group. A group is a big thing. A group is begun for definite *concerted* work, for a definite aim. I should have to trust you in this work and you would have to trust me and one another. Then it would be a group. Until there is general work it will be only a preparatory group. We shall prepare ourselves so as in the course of time to become a group by imitating a group...imitating it inwardly of course.

The manifesto of this period was the booklet entitled *The Rajneesh Foundation*. It was a time to relate openly: "be alert, let it happen".

5. *The World-Vision Period: Zorba the Buddha.* 1977-80. This period dates from the message to the Conference on Humanity's Future and stresses "the new man" as necessary to planetary survival. Initiation into neo-sannyas exploded from 20,000 to over 200,000 in a few years. The ashram increasingly was seen not only as a greenhouse for individual spiritual growth, but as a model commune, a world pattern—the basic, alternative, exemplary building-block of a new decentralized world order, the living embodiment of the social forms of a new, spiritual world.

What Prof. Charlie Fischer of Brandeis has called "social yoga", begun in the previous period, intensified now. This involved compassion, but defined as "doing whatever is necessary to bring awareness to the situation out of deep love and without an emotional charge behind it". Like Jesus with the whip, people were learning to give "hits". Later at the Ranch any social exchange became, potentially, an occasion for being told by someone or other that you were not being "right on". Of course, *they*, too, might be "off" in telling you this. All this came naturally out of sannyas, encounter and Gestalt groups, plus Osho's own direct truthfulness—thus, the reputation, later in the US, for sannyasins having "a confrontational style". How to be gentle yet frank?

At the same time, the organization was rapidly expanding and some were rising to high positions by fascistically rewarding insecure people into grateful obedience. This period also saw the search for a large tract of land in India. It ended with a government ban on the Gujarat purchase, Osho's back ailment, and the trip to America in May, 1981.

This was a time of pooling talents, creating big departments, programs. It was a time of learning to live and work together— and of not learning that Osho really *did* give dangerous freedom to people to make mistakes, and they needed much more watching than people, intently busy with working on themselves, knew. It was the time of the rise of Sheela.

6. *Buddhafield, Silent Communion, and Total Work as Meditation.* 1981-1984, the first phase of Rajneeshpuram, Oregon. The Ranch brought a whole host of new interconnected themes: World festivals, the way of the heart, the twenty-four mile Buddhafield, ecology, the AIDS warning, "carshan" drive-bys, the approaching world crisis and the Noah's Ark of consciousness, and Rajneeshism as the somewhat laconically conceived new religion to counter state and Federal efforts to destroy the Ranch. Groups resumed, Rajneesh International University was handsomely housed. Unchecked, the smiling, efficient "Ma-archy", grew ominously closed.

Continuities and discontinuities in the movement are hard to trace in this period because of the sheer blur of exploding construction projects: dams, sewage systems, irrigation, water and road systems, electricity and offices, stores and houses, garages and bus system, dairy farming, truck farming, recycling, stream reclamation, cattle ranching—a town from scratch in two years, synthesis of urban area, town, farm and wilderness in creative supplementation instead of competition. I suppose the manifesto of this period had to be the weekly *The Rajneesh*

Times, uneven as it was. Time to learn about power trips—the world's *and* ours.

This period of building ended abruptly in the middle of The Share-A-Home program when Bhagwan broke his three year silence and resumed talking, October 30, 1984. It had been as much of "the great experiment" as construction craziness allowed—demonstrating to the world a people somehow managing to live together in "love, life, laughter", making work into play, voluntarily cooperating, staying from love of Bhagwan.

7. *The Trashing Period: Anti Religion, Saviours, the State Sovereignty System, the Family*. 1984-87. This period saw the creation of *The Rajneesh Bible*, an all out attack on the conflict-ridden, sterile, anti-feminine past of humanity. Priests and politicians—the mafia of the soul. In part this attack, begun in the fall of 1984, may have been in response the anti-cult, anti-foreign, neo-populist culture of crackdown in the Reagan 80s. The Moral Majority became a significant political force. Drugs, drinking, Libya, spies, liberalism—everything that appeared lax or immoral—came under strange attack. America was changing.

Meanwhile the Ranch, hemmed in by discrimination of county, state and federal levels, legally attacked by environmental groups, local prejudice, mass media, the INS, and the state attorney general, was shaken to its roots by the departure of Sheela and her inner circle amid charges of attempted murder in defense of the Ranch, but also against Bhagwan's inner circle. Bhagwan invited a full investigation of Sheela's crimes, but the government ransacked files and investigated ways to end the ranch instead. The criminals were left largely alone, the ranch wasn't.

Amid rumours of a national guard takeover, a violent arrest of Bhagwan, fears of shooting, and chaos in work at the Ranch, tension peaked near the end of October, 1985. To cool things off, it was decided to take Bhagwan for a time to the North Carolina home of a relative of his new secretary, Ma Prem Hasya. Upon landing in Charlotte, however, Bhagwan was arrested without a warrant for "fleeing" an indictment that hadn't been published, and which, being Federal, was as valid in North Carolina as in Oregon, and so hadn't been "fled". In the final indictment, after other charges were dropped, he was accused of a crime for which no one else had ever been prosecuted: harbouring a thought in his mind to try to stay in this country when he asked to have his tourist visa extended three months! In such a case, just deporting would suffice. Instead, the last moves in four years of legal harassment were at hand.

For this heretofore unprosecuted, trivial crime, he was denied bail, jailed 12 days, kept in chains eleven hours, signed into a Oklahoma prison under the name of David Washington, roughed up, probably poisoned, and then left in an evacuated building during a bomb scare. His attorneys were then told he would be denied bail during an entire, lengthy trial and his safety in jail could not be guaranteed. His lawyers, partly because of these events and partly because of his allergies and diabetic condition, advised him to enter an Alford plea, accept a small fine, leave the country, and relocate the commune somewhere more congenial. He was fined $400,000.00. When he left the U.S., however, dis-information transmitted *via* diplomatic telex resulted in his expulsion from 20 countries. And U.S. planes somehow always landed near Bhagwan's plane, just as they had flown reconnaissance over the Ranch, once with Attorney General Edwin Meese aboard. Uruguay, which was willing to entertain the commune, was finally forced to deport Bhagwan in mid 1986 or lose U.S. foreign aid. The government didn't just want him out of the country, they wanted him silenced (as Meese declared), and the commune's example destroyed. Sannyasins then experienced difficulty getting into India. After a stay in Bombay, this period ended with the return to Poona. Prophetically important themes in this period were the manifesto on human rights and Gorbachev, the right man at the right time.

We should not leave this period without three observations. First, the ranch represented the largest utopian venture in Western history; and second, it was unique in basing itself, not on one of a hundred Western ideologies, but on meditational growth. Here the age-old Asian preoccupation with meditation and the age-old Western pursuit of utopia met, joined hands and worked together.

Another observation might be in order: the ranch did not blow up from within over money, sex or power as have most other Western utopias. It probably could have ridden out even Sheela's disgrace. In the end, it was crushed from without by the Attorney General's office, which forbid the INS to prosecute its flimsy case, and stepped in to manage the climactic events itself. People wonder why the ranch ended so swiftly and search for deep sociological reasons. The answer is fairly simple. Like the marines in Lebanon, the Ranch was hit by hardball opposition and driven out. Yet in a real sense the commune, while crushed in Oregon, has not ended. Some have relocated in Poona, while others live in the *diaspora*, waiting for a new commune to form around Osho Rajneesh. This was a difficult time of learning about living back in the world, about lingering attachments to old religious and family patterns, or returning to former professions, private lifestyles, personal weaknesses, growth.

8. *Yah Hoo, Yah Boo, the Mystic Rose and Zen: The Present Period.* 1987-1989. The themes of this period are the refusal to be silenced, deepening meditation, a new vision of women's liberation, the museum of ancient gods, the ecological crisis, and above all, Zen. Besides the new stress on planetary death, the old theme of the family as transmitter of all that is ugly in history has been intensified. Priests, politicians, and the State have all come under new attack. Meritocracy has been offered to transform the power-holders in democracy. Russia was warned that it has a spiritual vacuum that should be filled with something like Zen, not the old religions clamouring for re-legalization in *peristroika*.

At long last a complete break with the Hindu tradition came in dropping "Bhagwan Shree" from his name. The break with the Buddhist tradition came in dropping the short-lived names of Guatama the Buddha (and his ghost) and Zorba the Buddha. Now he is Osho Rajneesh, free of any tradition. Osho is a Japanese word for a master teacher of meditation.

Disciples continue to flock from all over the world, especially Germany and the Far East. Poona hosts up to 10,000 people at a time. Groups continue in the "Poona Program", music flourishes. The mystic rose twenty-one meditation group has seven days of laughing, seven for crying and seven for Vipassana. In Discourse, Osho leads concluding meditations. Many books appeared about Bhagwan—Strelley, Milne, Forman, Meredith,

Gordon and Murphy—three "for", three against. A flood of discourse books have been published, including ones on Kahlil Gibran and Nietzsche. Discourses were often twice daily. The thallium poison, after severe illnesses, seems to have worked its painful way out of Osho's body with perhaps residual damage to his eyes and immune system. The positive emphasis has been on the Golden Future and the World Academy of constructive science free of government control. Increasingly the emphasis has been that problems of population, war and environment are international and cannot be solved nationally. The manifestos of this period are a video called *The Manifesto*, and *The Golden Future*. The vision of the commune continues—replace society, *Gesellschaft*, with human sized, decentralized, soft technology communities, *Gemeinschaft*. The hope remains for the birth of a new man who, through meditation, will be able to live creatively together in communes, an exemplary pattern which might help end the sad, self-destructing, modern arrangement known as "society" and usher in a sustainable future, balanced with earth. It is, it seems, a time for waiting and for learning deeper meditation.

4

THERAPEUTIC ASPECTS OF NEW RELIGIOUS MOVEMENTS

Frederick Bird
and
Rooshikumar Pandya

The contemporary interest in New Religious Movements has been occasioned by a number of factors including the pursuit of therapeutic benefits. Large numbers of people have participated in these movements often for only short periods of time in order, among other reasons, to overcome feelings of depression, social isolation and lack of personal direction. Many participants claim that as a result of their involvements, they feel happier, more able to relate successfully with others, and clearer about their lives. (Anthony et al., 1977; Galanter, 1982; Heelas, 1982; Hill, 1980; Levine and Salter, 1976; Richardson, 1983; Westley, 1983). Although these movements similarly emphasize their therapeutic aspects, their approaches to therapy are often quite different. In fact these movements exhibit as varied approaches to therapy as they do to religion. In this paper we examine three different approaches to group therapy adopted by New Religious Movements. These approaches have as well been adopted by both traditional religious groups and by secular therapies. We examine the typical strategies of each approach as well as the corresponding consequences for those involved.

Variations in Therapy and Religion

Following Frank, we use the term therapy to refer broadly to activities intentionally organized for this purpose, which enable men and women to feel less distressed and less demoralized about themselves and to function more easily and effectively in their social relationships. We further stipulate that these activities constitute therapies only insofar as they focus on a personal relationship (usually of limited duration), the particular character of personal distresses are diagnosed and specific remedies are then pursued (Frank, 1963, Chapters 1,2,4). Defined in these terms, many New Religions utilize therapeutic techniques. For comparative purposes, it is possible to identify three approaches to therapy fostered by these groups: namely interactional, healthy-minded, and retreat-taking.

Interactional therapies use various group exercises to facilitate clearer, more direct communications between people. These communications become a means for individuals to practice expressing their own feelings and attending to the feelings of others, while avoiding their ordinary defenses. Participants are encouraged to look at problems in new ways both by imaginatively taking on the roles of others and thinking of themselves in different ways. Participants are frequently encouraged to offer testimonials in which they recount their difficulties and their progress in relation to group objectives (Schwartz, 1977). Often these therapies challenge participants to establish various short run goals, such as reducing food intake, abstaining from alcohol, become more assertive, or more directly expressing emotions (Glasser, 1965). Group leaders are expected to play the role of facilitators, teaching group members new exercises, fostering lively interactions, and calling members back to their tasks when they get distracted. Interaction therapies have been especially championed by the encounter group movement (Bach, 1972; Oden, 1982). Imaginative, sometimes exotic interaction therapies have also been fostered by groups like Psychosynthesis, Arica, EST, the School of Economic Science and Shakti, all of which have incorporated religious elements in their programs (Westley, 1983; Palmer, 1978; Hounan and Hogg, 1984).

Healthy-minded therapies use techniques to help individuals cultivate a state of mind that is viewed as an internal source of healing power. The purpose of these techniques is not immediately to facilitate more skill at interactions but to develop a personal competency to identify and to utilize creative life forces within. In order to develop this competency, participants characteristically are trained to distance themselves from life-denying forces. They learn to practice detachment from factors that are likely to distract them, to make them anxious and agitated and to provoke stress. Sometimes they are directly challenged to undertake with equanimity and inner poise tasks that otherwise might upset them in order to practice developing this inner sense of calm detachment. Sometimes they are cautioned to avoid such disturbing activities altogether. Healthy-minded therapies make use of diverse meditational practices in order to help individuals cultivate inner peace, often using breathing techniques, mantras, and mandalas. Many healthy-minded therapies train participants to recognize, cultivate and utilize their own internal healing powers. This healing power is usually associated with the internal states of mind reached by meditation but may more popularly be characterized as a positive state of mind (James, 1901:78-114). Leaders of healthy-minded therapies usually act as initiators, leading participants into new, heretofore undiscovered, dimensions of themselves. Healthy minded therapies have been used by traditional mind-cure groups, like Christian Science, by theosophical groups like Gurdjieff followers, and by contemporary movements like Silva Mind Control and Transcendental Meditation.

As an approach to therapy retreat-taking emphasizes the benefits that result from fully, imaginatively, and playfully taking breaks from ordinary responsibilities and activities and entering upon alternatives that are re-creational in the root meaning of that phrase. Retreat-taking may be contracted for like rest and relaxation excursions by making arrangements with retreat centres, health spas, guided cruises, holiday camps, or educational institutes. Such centres use eclectic assortments of techniques that create the sense of living in an alternative milieu that are at once peaceful, engaging, exotic, challenging, adventuresome and personally accepting. The techniques themselves usually include comparatively strenuous or at least demanding physical exercises, sundry forms of play-therapy, instructional classes and periods for meditation. Whatever techniques are used the objective is to foster total involvement for a period of time, from as short as a weekend or consecutive weekends, to longer stretches. The aim is to allow and demand that participants bracket the ordinary concerns that weigh them down and encourage other interests, desires, fantasies to take seed and grow. Retreat therapies have been developed by many groups like the Rajneesh movement, Sivananda Yoga, the Naropa Institute, as well as various secular retreat centres.

These approaches to therapy are distinctly different but not mutually exclusive. The interactional approach seeks to help people directly improve their skills at interpersonal relations. The healthy minded approach seeks alternatively to help people directly alter their own self images by acknowledging and utilizing personal resources which had been previously unrecognized. Retreat-makers emphasize the therapeutic benefits from stepping outside ordinary roles and imaginatively and playfully experiencing alternatives.

It is impossible to gauge the impact of these different therapeutic approaches among new religions without taking into account as well the different approaches to religion which these groups favour. Variations in the ways of being religious influence the ways particular therapeutic approaches are treated.

Initially we had hoped to observe what differences religious convictions made by comparing contemporary religious and non-religious groups which incorporate therapies. Our research demonstrated that such determinations are very difficult because of the considerable variation in both the ways and the degree to which contemporary therapy groups and New Religious Movements are religious. Groups like Transcendental Meditation incorporate ancient Hindu rituals and beliefs, and present themselves publicly as non-religious. Groups like Scientology utilize modern psychological testing devices and techniques, and present themselves publicly as religious.

For the purpose of this research, we distinguished a number of different ways of being religious. What distinguishes these types is differences in ways adherents relate to what they regard as sacred. In some groups adherents act as apprentices to shaman/priests who introduce them to sacred mysteries. As apprentices they learn skills which in time they can use, if they become proficient, to act like shamans themselves, using healing powers for their own or others' benefits. Apprentice-like relationships are found in groups like Psychosynthesis, Silva Mind Control and Shakti. In other groups participants act like devotees of exemplary prophets, who are often regarded like avatars as mediating embodiments of sacred reality. Adherents seek to imitate their leaders whom they regard as extraordinary, enlightened beings. Devotee-like relationships are found in groups like Divine Light, the Unification Church and the followers of Swami Shyam. Participants in a number of groups act like disciples of a sacred discipline, cultivating their own inner powers by gaining competency through spiritual and physical exercises. They regard their teachers as revered masters, who have themselves excelled as students of their sacred disciplines. Disciple-like relationships are found in groups like Tai Chi Chu'an, Zen centres, and many Yoga groups. In addition to these three types, which have been discussed before (Bird and Reimer, 1982), two additional types are identifiable. Participants at the peripheries of a number of groups and at the core of a few groups act like clients seeking spiritual aid from sacred spirits by means of mediums or shamans. They do not seek to establish an immediate enduring relationship of their own. Rather, often in response to a particular problem, they seek temporary aid from someone skilled at contacting sacred realities. Client-like relationships are characteristic of Spiritualist groups (Bird and Westley, 1985). Finally, adherents in other groups act as worshippers, revering and seeking the care of sacred transcendent beings. Leaders of these groups function like priests, guiding the ritual activities, which usually represent the sacred being in their midst. Worshipper-like relationships are found in groups such as Krishna Consciousness, Shinran Buddhists, and Charismatics. This typology is not meant to be exhaustive or final. It is drawn in order to characterize the variety of ways of being religious in New Religious Movements. This typology is set forth as well in order to gauge how differences in religious orientations combine with differences in therapeutic approaches.

In this article we are primarily interested in gauging the significance of these different therapeutic approaches. We have not, therefore, attempted to explore the many different ways in which these approaches to therapy and religious orientations have been combined. Rather, we have chosen to examine more closely three groups in each of which one therapeutic approach has been given prominence. Two of these groups are new religious movements: Creative Awareness and local followers of Rajneesh. The third group, Transactional Analysis, is secular, even though the participants in this group more readily identify themselves as being religious than do the Rajneesh followers. The Transactional Analysis group uses an interaction approach to therapy in a non-religious environment. Creative Awareness uses a healthy-minded approach to therapy in a religious group in which adherents treat themselves as apprentices cultivating shaman-like skills. A sizeable proportion of the adherents of both groups, apart from these groups, participate as worshippers in traditional, denominational religious groups. The Rajneesh movement has favoured a retreat-taking approach to therapy in a group at once religious and secular in which participants primarily acted like devotees of an exemplary prophet while cultivating various spiritual and physical disciplines.

The Three Groups

For the purpose of this study we submitted questionnaires to a random sample of the membership of a Creative Awareness group and a Sannyasin association in Montreal and a Transactional Analysis group in Toronto as well as a control group, selected from similarly aged persons. A total of 90 questionnaires were completed. The therapy group was comprised of individuals in two short term workshops, directed by a leader who uses the techniques and the philosophy of Transactional Analysis.

The Creative Awareness group combines both religious and therapeutic features in its practice and philosophy. It is led by an Anglican clergyman; it uses religious terms in its statements; and it identifies its aims in relation to spiritual development and devotion to God. At the same time, the group represents an offshoot from the movement of Mind Control started by Jose

Silva. One of the ostensible aims of the group is to help persons become functioning psychics and to use this power in a healing fashion to help others. The Sannyasin group is made up of followers of the contemporary guru, Mohan Rajneesh, who has developed his own philosophy from bits of Taoism, Tantrism, Hindu philosophy and western psychology. This movement began in India in 1974. It has quickly developed and attracted large numbers of Indian, European, and North American followers. Originally Rajneesh established a commune/ashram in Poona, India, near Bombay. More recently he established a centre in Antelope, Oregon. Rajneesh, who is considered to be an embodiment of deity by his followers, instructed his disciples to undertake a discipline of regular meditation, to follow a vegetarian diet, and to enhance their inner freedom. He views various therapies as ancillary supports for his programs.

The Transactional Analysis group performed several therapeutic functions for participants. As a result of their involvement, participants felt that both the extent and the intensity of their personal distress becomes markedly reduced. Similarly, their sense of social isolation was diminished and their own sense of purpose and personal direction were enhanced. Before entering this group almost all participants complained of feeling nervous and tense, depressed and glum, and uncertain and unclear about how to lead their lives. Two thirds complained of emotional problems. In comparison to controls, TA participants were two to three times as likely to complain of these kinds of personal distress. Clearly these were people who had not been happy and had not been managing their lives very well. Participants claimed that their involvement with the group has greatly improved their feelings about themselves. They claimed that they felt less tense, less depressed, and less unclear about their lives as a result of their participation. They felt that their emotional problems had been greatly reduced and they had been able to develop closer relationships with others (Tables 1).

The Transactional Analysis group helped its participants in two ways in particular. One, it provided a context where persons openly and non-judgmentally talked with others about some of their personal problems. What participants especially valued about the TA group was that it established a social milieu in which persons could listen to the experiences of others, casually socialize, and share their own burdens with others. Participants in the TA group felt they understood others better and were closer to them as a result of their involvement although to a degree comparable to the two religious groups. However, in contrast with members of both religious groups, TA participants were much more likely to value the group because of the way in which this listening and speaking to others about personal problems and concerns helped them to think and decide more clearly. The therapy group helped these persons, so they said, not by giving them direction for life and not by enabling them to attain higher states of consciousness but by allowing them to air their feelings and thereby to feel better about themselves (Table 2 and 3). Two, TA participants testified that their involvement with this group especially benefited them by enabling them to find greater satisfaction in their interpersonal relationships. In part, the group facilitated this end by providing a setting where persons could initiate new friendships. While only 40% of participants claimed to have close friends before entering the group, 86% said that they had close friends after their involvement. Overall, then, the TA group served as a temporary catalyst which improved both participants' personal sense of well-being and effectiveness and the enjoyment with which they interacted with others.

The group leader, a professional therapist, played a central role in this process. Participants clearly and enthusiastically valued her work. In comparison to how they viewed their parents, participants were much more likely to view her as being self-confident, loving, attractive, trustworthy, and non-judgmental. And they were less likely to view her as being critical and manipulative (see Table 5). TA participants in particular valued their leader because of her empathy and because of the constructive criticism which she gave them. Similarly while less than one fourth of the other two groups valued their leaders as sources of constructive criticism, more than half of the TA participants identified this trait as a particular strength of their leader. Still, TA participants were less willing to over-idealize their leaders. She was, they claimed, loving, easy to talk to, and an ideal person. However, unlike the religious adherents, they hesitated to claim that she was "extremely" so.

TABLE ONE

FORMS OF SOCIAL RELATIONSHIPS BEFORE AND AFTER INVOLVEMENT WITH GROUP

TYPES OF SOCIAL RELATIONSHIPS	CREATIVE AWARENESS		SANNYASIN		TRANSACTIONAL ANALYSIS		CONTROL
	Before	After	Before	After	Before	After	Before
1 Had Close Friends	48%	72%	72%	88%	40%	86%	44%
2. Participated in Several Organizations	48%	52%	28%	24%	33%	20%	44%
N	25		25		15		25

1. Before S x C: $x^2 = 4.023$ (p <.05); S x TA: $x^2 = 4.000$ (p <.05)
Before/ TA: $x^2 = 7.033$ (p <.01)
After+

TABLE TWO

FEELINGS OF PERSONAL DISTRESS BEFORE AND AFTER INVOLVEMENT WITH GROUPS

TYPES OF DISTRESS	CREATIVE AWARENESS		SANNYASIN		TRANSACTIONAL ANALYSIS		CONTROL
	Before	After	Before	After	Before	After	Before
1. Felt Nervous and Tense	72%	12%	44%	16%	100%	38%	52%
2. Felt Depressed and Glum	56%	8%	40%	12%	80%	33%	32%
3. Felt Goals Unclear Re: Life	68%	12%	56%	40%	87%	27%	36%

4. Had Emotional Problems	52%	4%	20%	20%	67%	20%	16%
Mean		62	9	40	22	84	29	35
N		25		25		15		25

1. Before   TA x C:$x2=10.286$ (p <.01)
   Before/   CA:$x2=18.473$ (p <.001);   S: $x2=4.667$ (p <.05);
   After   TA:$x2=12,857$ (p <.001)

2. Before   TA x C:$x2=8.640$ (p <.01)
   Before/   CA:$x2=13.235$ (p <.01);   S: $x2=5.094$ (p <.05);
   After   TA:$x2=6.652$ (p <.01)

3. Before   CA x C:$x2=5.128$ (p <.05); S x C: $x2=6.876$ (p <.01);
                TA x C:$x2=16.835$ (p <.001)
   Before/   CA:$x2=16.333$ (p <.001);   TA: $x2=10.995$ (p <.01)
   After

4. Before   CA x C:$x2=7.219$ (p <.01); TA x C:$x2=10.579$ (p <.01)
   Before/   CA: $x2=14.286$ (p <.001);   TA: $x2=6.657$ (p <.01)
   After

The Creative Awareness fellowship identifies itself as a group which is at once both religious and therapeutic. To be sure, it does not consider itself to be a religion as such but rather a human growth movement with religious aspects. The movement is led by a priest and its ostensible aim is to help participants develop their spiritual powers. Of the various benefits which they have received from this group, adherents rank the two most important as "serving God" and "realizing their spiritual potential" (Table 3). 84% of the adherents of the Creative Awareness group claimed that their participation had made them feel closer to God. Only 20% of the TA participants made a similar claim. Creative Awareness members were no more "religious" than the participants in the TA therapy group as measured by their acknowledged religious affiliation and the extent to which they regularly participated in services of worship (Table 6). However, TA participants clearly differentiated their religious involvement from their therapeutic invclvement. In contrast, for CA adherents these involvements overlapped.

TABLE THREE

WAYS GROUPS ASSIST INDIVIDUALS	CREATIVE AWARENESS	SANNYASIN	TRANSACTIONAL ANALYSIS
1. Individual's Burdens Shared By All	28%	0%	60%
2. Understand Others Better; Feel Closer to Others	68%	44%	67%
3. Group Supports Decisions of Individual; Group Helps Individual to Think Clearly	28%	8%	53%
Mean	41%	17%	60%
N	25	25	15
1. CA x TA	$x^2=4.000$	$(p<.05)$	
2. S x TA	$x^2=9.355$	$(p<.001)$	
3. S x TA	$x^2=10.276$	$(p<.01)$	

Involvement with Creative Awareness had clear therapeutic benefits for participants. These benefits were not entirely accidental, since one of the primary aims of Creative Awareness is to help individuals develop healing powers for themselves and for others by learning how to make contact with spiritual powers within themselves. Before entering this group, in proportions equivalent to those entering the therapy group, they said they felt depressed and glum, suffered from emotional problems, felt tense and nervous, and were uncertain about the direction of their lives. Many felt friendless. Moreover, as a result of their involvement with this group, CA participants both felt decidedly better about themselves and had developed closer relationships with other persons (Table 1). In twice the proportion to adherents of other groups (83% compared to 46%), they felt happy after each meeting. In particular they felt they had grown because of their involvement; that they were more fulfilled as persons, and that they understood themselves better. They also felt they understood others better and were closer to them. Their scores with regard to these concerns were significantly higher than those for participants in the other two groups (Table 4).

TABLE FOUR

PRIMARY OBJECTIVES WHICH GROUPS HELP PARTICIPANTS TO REALIZE

Percentage of Respondents Selecting Following Objectives Among Top Four (Out of a List of Fifteen Objectives) in the Following Groups:

CREATIVE AWARENESS	SANNYASIN	TRANSACTIONAL ANALYSIS
1. To Realize Spiritual Potential (72%)	1. To Realize Spiritual Potential (71%)	1. To Find Satisfaction in my Family and Personal Relationship (80%)
2. To Serve God (60%)	2. To Become an Integrated Person (71%)	2. To Enjoy Myself (67%)
3. To Help Create A More Peaceful and A More Just World (60%)	3. To Reach a Higher State of Consciousness (71%)	3. To Become An Integrated Person (60%)
	4. To Enjoy Myself (60%)	

N.B. Just those objectives which received 60% affirmative response or more are listed above. The total list of objectives from which respondents could select were as follows: "To find satisfaction in my family and in my personal relationships", "to become an integrated person", "to help create a more peaceful and a more just world", "to serve God", "to realize spiritual potential", "to enjoy myself", "to reach a higher state of consciousness" (all the above were named by at least 60% of respondents in one of the three groups). Other objectives not selected by proportions that large included the following: "to achieve success in my career", "to find satisfaction in my work", "to live in turn with nature", "to help others fulfil themselves", "to achieve autonomy", "to improve my decision-making ability", "to achieve a feeling of self-worth", and "other".

The Creative Awareness group helped participants to achieve these kinds of therapeutic benefits by means quite different than those practised in the TA group. Participants did say that they especially benefited from self-awareness and relaxation exercises, exercises which are employed by many therapy groups. But they also testified that in addition they found prayer, worship and meditation especially helpful. (Table 2). Adherents benefited from a variety of religious and non-religious therapeutic practices which variously served as a means by which they developed closer contact with what they described as self-transcending spiritual realities. These spiritual realities were at once associated with God and with higher, spiritual dimensions of the self. These spiritual realities were envisioned to be mediums by means of which persons might attain closer, more beneficial relations with others, with oneself, and with God. CA participants identified three goals which their group most helped them to achieve: these goals were "serving God", helping them to "realize their spiritual potential" and helping them to "create a more peaceful world" (Table 3). For participants in this group, the "spiritual" evidently was related to other self-transcending realities, like "God" and "world peace".

Members of the CA groups were far more inclined to believe that both suffering and good fortune occurred to people because of the influence of various self-transcending spiritual realities. In at least twice the proportions of other respondents, they believed a person's fortunes were determined at least in part by forces like "the devil", "karma" and "disobeying God". To be sure, in ways similar to other respondents, they fatalistically felt that a person's destiny was rarely influenced by his or her own will power, but that it was often markedly influenced by what certain significant others—people in power and parents—did or did not do (Table 7). CA participants thus assumed a pluralistic vision of the world in which spiritual forces also played a part but in which they as persons played a limited role. It is reasonable to conjecture that they held these beliefs prior to their involvement with Creative Awareness. They had what Lofland and Stark have referred to as a "religious problem-solving orientation" (Lofland and Stark, 1973:38-47) and the CA group confirmed their perspective on the world but made these pluralistic forces seem less erratic and made participants feel more powerful. By means of the practices of meditation, self-awareness exercises, worship and prayer, as well as relaxation exercises, participants were able to develop their own spiritual powers and thereby develop a more lively and reassuring sense of inter-connection with other persons and with God.

Thus when CA participants claimed that their involvement with this group enabled them to know themselves and others better, to feel both more fulfilled and closer to others, it was not because they had gained more information about themselves and others nor because they had directly worked on improving their relationships with others or their feelings about themselves. The CA group did not directly focus on these matters. These benefits were by-products that occurred indirectly as CA helped participants to gain a new sense of themselves and their world. Creative Awareness helped participants see themselves as persons with spiritual powers. Initially the group showed them how these powers might be used telepathically to transmit healing energies to others. They learned that these powers might also be employed to facilitate more harmonious relations with others. As a consequence of these beliefs, CA adherents began to perceive their inter-personal relationships somewhat differently. They did not need to feel as wary of others. They might, they believed, in their own way by spiritual means influence others, at least to the extent of attempting to render them more peaceful and well-meaning. Their fatalistic anxieties were reduced. They sensed an interconnection between themselves and others, in which they could act as causal agents, not directly by will power and by public and historically acknowledged means, but indirectly by spiritual means. Through meditation, by learning to relax, and by detaching their affective sense of well-being from secular instances of success and failure, participants felt less vulnerable to the adverse influence of others and more able to act positively on their own behalf.

Like the participants in the other two groups surveyed, CA adherents held their leader in high regard. However, in about the same proportions they viewed their parents as having been, and their leaders as being "judgemental" (Tables 5). Considering that CA adherents otherwise have such high regard for their leader, this evaluation at first seems puzzling. However, the Creative Awareness leader does not act as facilitator for an encounter, for which some measure of non-judgemental empathy is necessary. Rather, he acts as a shaman/priest initiating devotees into a mystery. His role was dogmatically to insist upon a particular view of the world and then to introduce initiates into this world by following a prescribed set of techniques. Still, while he played this priestly role, he was not viewed as an avatar. It was possible to criticize him just as it was possible to criticize parents. Moreover, CA participants were cautioned to be no more dependent upon him than they were on parents. He had taught them some techniques and methods, which they in turn could utilize on their own. The group provided a context for reaffirming their beliefs and for practising meditation. It was the group rather than the leader to which they remained connected.

TABLE FIVE

COMPARISON OF THE PERCENTAGE OF RESPONDENTS REGARDING THEIR LEADERS AS BEING EITHER EXTREME OR ORDINARY EMBODIMENTS OF SELECTED ATTRIBUTES

ATTRIBUTES AND DEGREE OF EMBODIMENT	CREATIVE	SANNYASIN	TRANSACTIONAL
(1) Easy to Talk to			
(a) Extremely So	44	68	33
(b) Ordinarily So	32	12	54
(c) Total	76	80	87
(2) Loving			
(a) Extremely So	44	92	20
(b) Ordinarily So	20	4	60
(c) Total	64	96	80
N	25	25	15

1(a) S x TA: $x2=4.552$ ($p < .05$)
2(c) S x TA: $x2=21.363$ ($p < .001$)

The Sannyasin group, comprised of local followers of Mohan Rajneesh, is a religious group with therapeutic aspects. The group possesses unmistakable religious features. The leader claims to be an avatar, a living embodiment of sacred reality. Furthermore, he articulates a philosophy that combines elements of Taoism, Hinduism, Tantrism and Zen. Adherents claim that the group aids them most by helping them to realize more fully their spiritual potential. However, at the same time as they are describing their group in these terms, the Sannyasin members speak as if their group were not really religious, at least not in a denominational sense. 70% of them listed their religious identification as "none". More than others surveyed, they have renounced the religious identifications with which they grew up. Yet, in spite of these evident disclaimers, 60% of the Sannyasin members participate in services of worship at least several times a month (Table 6). Moreover, although they claimed that they found prayer without utility, they claimed that both chanting and meditating were of considerable benefit (Table 2).

TABLE SIX

COMPARISON OF THE PERCENTAGE OF RESPONDENTS ASSIGNING SELECTED ATTRIBUTES TO PARENTS AND LEADERS

ATTRIBUTES	CREATIVE AWARENESS		SANNYASIN		TRANSACTIONAL ANALYSIS		CONTROLS
	P	L	P	L	P	L	Parents
(1) Empathetic	48%	40%	44%	44%	40%	80%	44%
(2) Critical	72%	28%	60%	32%	40%	20%	52%
(3) Manipulative	28%	44%	52%	12%	40%	27%	23%
N	25	25	25	25	15	15	25

Participants expressed similar ambivalence with regard to the therapeutic aspects of their group. They described themselves as not being especially distressed or socially isolated prior to their involvement with the Sannyasin group. In proportions similar to controls (Sannyasin 20%, Control 17%), they denied having any emotional problems. Although to a greater extent they admitted to feelings of depression (40%) and tension (44%), their responses corresponded again to those of the controls (Table 1). Although few participated in several social organizations, they claimed to be highly involved in interpersonal friendships and gatherings (Table 1). Yet, other responses from Sannyasin participants indicated that they were not as happy with their lives as they would like, nor as involved in their own future as they might be. More than half of the Sannyasins felt unclear about how to lead their lives. This was a ratio much higher than for controls (Table 1). To a greater degree than for other respondents they had developed an experimental life style: 40% had previously been involved in other new religious movements and 47% had been high on marijuana several times. Considerably more than for other respondents, Sannyasin members exhibited an absence of what might be described as social rootedness. Although their mean age, as for control, was in the lower 30's, they had much less committed themselves to establishing families of their own. Over 60% were single, separated or divorced. They were much less likely to be involved in social organizations than all other respondents (Table 1). On the basis of this evidence, it seems reasonable to conclude that Sannyasin members were not succeeding as well as most of their similarly-aged peers in assuming adult like involvements in relation to family, careers, and community. This may well have engendered in them feelings of inadequacy and directionlessness. However, these feelings were evidently difficult for them to acknowledge, directly and openly.

Sannyasins obtained from their involvement with this group a therapeutic benefit, which might best be described as the enhanced feeling of self-approval and self-worth. It is possible to get a sense of what they felt they got from the group, by noting first what they claimed not to have obtained. They argued that their emotional problems were not greatly lessened but they had not been very marked in the first place. In sharp contrast to TA participants, they denied that the group helped them to make decisions and to think clearly. Nor did they feel, as TA participants did, appreciably closer and more involved with others (Tables 4). Their involvement with the Sannyasin group had not led them to become more socially rooted. Nor had it enhanced their sense of control or influence over others (Table 7). If anything, their involvement with Rajneesh's movement seems to have confirmed and validated a personal sense of distance from others and from the authoritative claims of others about their lives.In ways that we need to analyze further, by submitting to the particular kind of authority exercised by Rajneesh,

TABLE SEVEN

COMPARISON OF THE PERCENTAGE OF RESPONDENTS IDENTIFYING LEADERS AND PARENTS AS EXTREME EMBODIMENTS OF SELECTED ATTRIBUTES

	CREATIVE AWARENESS		SANNYAS		INTRANSACTIONAL ANALYSIS		CONTROLS
	P	L	P	L	P	L	Parents
1 Easy To Talk To	16	44	16	68	20	33	20
2. Loving	28	44	32	92	27	20	28
3. Self-Confident	16	48	32	84	7	53	24
4. Non-Judgemental	16	16	4	76	33	20	16
Mean	19	38	21	80	22	32	22
N	25		25		15		25

Sannyasin members felt freer to reduce the aura of legitimacy attached to authoritative directions and critiques of others (see Bird, 1978). These feelings are especially evident in relation to their contrasting attitudes towards their parents and their leader. In very large proportions, greatly exceeding the regard of other participants, they viewed Rajneesh as being extremely "loving", "self-confident", "easy to talk to", and "non-judgemental". While they assessed their parents with regard to these attributes similarly to all other respondents, the contrasting views of the leader and their parents were much more marked (Tables 5). In their idealization of Rajneesh they indirectly expressed decisively disenchanted feelings about their parents, especially with regard to the ease and the unjudgemental attitudes with which they could talk with them. Following Rajneesh allowed them to distance themselves from the judgemental attitudes both of their parents, and, no doubt, themselves as well. Correspondingly, by distancing themselves from others and from the authoritative claims of others over their lives, they allowed themselves to feel better about themselves.

This conclusion is confirmed by analyzing the claims that Sannyasin members made about the direct benefits of their involvement. They identified four benefits as being especially valued, namely: helping them to realize their spiritual potential, helping them to become integrated persons, helping them to obtain higher states of consciousness, and helping them to enjoy themselves more (Table 3). When these benefits are analyzed together, then a particular composite picture emerges of the ideal image that Sannyasins hold of themselves. Their involvement in this group enabled them to achieve what they refer to as a higher, more spiritual, and also by implication a more morally neutral view of themselves. By quieting their own internal judgmental voices, they have gained a greater sense of integration and they enjoy themselves more. The word "spiritual" possesses quite different meaning for Sannyasin members than for Creative Awareness participants. It does not refer to self-transcending powers that people can utilize to overcome the sense of distance between persons. It refers rather to a peaceful, undistressed state of mind, not overly disturbed by the claims and authoritative judgements of others and self. While TA participants also value the benefits of personal integration and self-enjoyment, they decisively connect these objectives to the goal of developing satisfactory relationships with others. Sannyasin members in contrast view self-integration in a context which emphasizes their distance from others, like family members, professional colleagues, parents and other group members, which might make claims upon their lives.

It is not surprising that Sannyasin members admit to feeling less tense and nervous, less depressed and glum as a consequence of their participation (Table 1). However, they were noticeably reluctant to define these benefits as personal growth (Table 4). After all, to admit that one has grown is to further confess that one needed to grow and that one had been in some ways immature. Participants in both the TA group and the Creative Awareness Fellowship readily made this confession. Sannyasin members in contrast did not. Moreover, their response in this regard is consistent with other aspects of their involve ment. Growth is associated with change. Sannyasin members say that their involvement in this group has not occasioned changes in their lives with regard to emotional problems, clarity about life goals, social rootedness, the understanding of others, and the closeness of their relationship with others.

While their involvement may not occasion personal growth for adherents, it does seem to provide a context in which adherents can experience what Erikson once referred to as a social and psychological moratorium on expectations with regard to growth (Erikson, 1968). Erikson used this term to refer to the years of late adolescence and early adulthood during which persons distanced themselves from various commitments and identifications in order to increase their sense of personal space in relation to which their own sense of identity might emerge. As Erikson has demonstrated in his studies of both Luther and Gandhi, some persons may delay resolving this identity crisis, particularly when questions of identity become over-charged with questions about personal authenticity and integrity. Such persons may distance themselves from their social environment—Luther joined a monastic order, Gandhi sojourned in England and South Africa—until such time as their own sense of personal identity emerges (Erikson, 1958; Erikson, 1969). Some persons may never re-attach themselves to their social environment. They may attempt to resolve their identity crisis negatively by establishing both social and psychological distances from others. The Sannyasin group appears to encourage this kind of detachment or distancing.

Sannyasin members achieve this sense of detachment and well-being by several means. In part the practice of meditation itself facilitates these ends by placing persons repeatedly in a situation where they put themselves at a distance from extraneous demands and expectations on their lives by identifying themselves with a higher, transcendent self-observing aspect of themselves. Partly the Sannyasin group fosters these ends by providing an opportunity for individuals to take a break from ordinary routines while attending the centres which Rajneesh has established. Attending these centres is much like going off for a summer camp experience: There is some discipline, mixed with recreational activities, work, rituals, and a good deal of camraderie. It is a kind of extended liminal experience with the corresponding feelings of humanity and community and without much personal accountability. It may well be recreational in the best sense of the word (Turner, 1964).

To a large extent this socially detached sense of personal well-being is fostered and supported by the relationship which members develop with the leader, Mohan Rajneesh. Members clearly idealize this man and identify with him. In spite of the fact that Rajneesh has written dozens of books, it is not his words but his example that is important for followers. He exhibits vitality, humour, self-command, non-conformity, and independence of mind. He is eminently self-confident. Although he is a man of many and decided views, to his followers he appears to be especially non-judgemental. These features appear to be particularly important. The extent to which Sannyasin members view him as being an attractive and loving person seems to be related to the degree to which they view him as well to be self-confident and non-judgemental (Table 5). Rajneesh's followers value him so greatly in a large part because of the example he sets of a man who with self-assured authority follows his own inner genius and feels certain about himself. Their identification with him seems to serve, as Freud once argued more generally with regard to charismatic leaders of social movements, as an antidote to otherwise quite powerful feelings of melancholy (Freud,

1921). Melancholy results, Freud argued, from a felt discrepancy between one's self and the objects of one's identification, which ordinarily are one's parents. Unable or unwilling to adhere to parental expectations and model—either because of their own sense of inadequacy or because of the inadequacy of their parents—Sannyasin members seem to experience strong feelings of self-criticism. These latter feelings appear to be overcome by identifying instead with an alternative ego ideal, who by being loving, self-assured and non-judgemental, does not engender these melancholic moods.

Conclusions

Many new religious movements have incorporated one or more of these therapeutic approaches. Interaction therapies most directly seek to change overt behavioural patterns. In experiencing settings they reward people for learning new, more beneficial ways of integrating with others and punish them for failing to learn. Although we examined the use of this approach in a non-religious group, a number of contemporary religious groups have adopted interaction therapies. Psychosynthesis uses interaction therapies in a group in which members are treated as apprentices, learning new psychic and interpersonal skills through various workshops and classes. Alcoholics Anonymous also employs interactional techniques like testimonials and group discussions together with prayers and worship-like rituals. While interaction techniques are used in non-religious and apprentice-type groups like Transactional Analysis and Psychosynthesis as part of temporary, short term programs of therapy, this approach is used to reinforce long term commitments among groups of worshippers, who revere self-transcending Sacred Others. For example, although AA does not identify itself as a distinct religion as such, and encourages participants to cultivate their independent religious commitments, through their own discussions and rituals they honour belief in God as a transcending caring being, able to strengthen individuals in their resolves by themselves and through the group. Similarly among Nichiren Buddhists, interaction techniques, like testimonials which often function like a role-playing device, function to strengthen the connections between members. Members expose their feelings and life histories to each other at the same time as they reconfirm their commitment to the sacred Buddhist Truth of the Lotus Sutra. However, in religious groups of worshippers like Nichiren Buddhists, only an abbreviated repertoire of interaction techniques are typically incorporated and these are subordinated to the worship and proselytizing aims of the group.

Healthy-minded therapies often possess a religious character because standardized techniques are used like revered rituals in order to give people more effective access to their own immanent healing powers. These powers are characteristically treated like sacred realities as being set apart, extraordinary, powerful, and accessible only through particular symbolic means (Westley, 1983). Healthy-minded therapies primarily function to augment individual self-confidence by enabling people to experience themselves as persons with the capacities to distance themselves from distracting attachments and to call upon their own heretofore latent psychic energies. Unlike interactionists, healthy-minded therapies do not directly diagnose and analyze the sources of personal distress in interactional processes or personal self-images. They believe that personal problems are not resolved by such analyses, which frequently only lead to further attachments to these problems. Rather, they attempt to help people experience themselves in new ways as bearers of their own healing powers.

This therapeutic approach has been incorporated into different religious patterns. In Christian Science this approach is combined with ordinary patterns of low liturgical Protestant worship. Therapeutic benefits are considered by-products of worshipping relationships. In Tibetan Buddhist groups and Tai Chi the healthy-minded mind set is cultivated as part of the discipline of meditation. Both groups emphasize detachment from unhealthy, life-denying phenomena along with the practice of centring one's mind by meditation exercises. In religious groups of worshippers and disciples, the healthy-minded therapies are incorporated with on-going patterns of commitment to a Sacred Other and community of worshippers and to the sacred disciplines and their community of disciples. In the Creative

Awareness group a healthy-minded approach to therapy was used as part of a training program during which, like sorcerer's apprentices, participants learned how to become functioning psychics. Commitment was for a short term, but Creative Awareness was not a therapy group as such. People did not initially participate in order to diagnose and cure their distresses. Indeed they claimed to receive therapeutic benefits but only as a byproduct of the training program. Their central objective was to acquire skills as agents of healing power.

The retreat-taking approach to therapy is the most eclectic in terms of techniques and methods. Typically this approach initially emphasizes recreational aspects as a means to re-fresh, re-juvenate, and renew oneself. However, when incorporated with religious movements, this approach often functions to reinforce commitments among group members at the same time that these practices also occasion therapeutic benefits. In this way modern retreat takers may function not dissimilarly to traditional camp meetings, which combined recreation with revivals.

As it has been incorporated within New Religious movements, retreat-taking as a therapeutic approach has assumed several forms. Sivananda Yoga, for example, directly recruits people to participate in vacation-like weekends or weeks in beautiful holiday settings. They depict themselves as an alternative to a Club Mediterranean vacation, in which a central core of disciplined meditation and hatha yoga will be combined with sports, vegetarian meals, inspirational talks, private devotions and exercises. In developing such programs, Sivananda Yoga seems to be encouraging contrasting developments: namely, both a greater commitment to the discipline of Yoga as well as individual's own autonomous discretion to utilize their services and vacation settings for their own private enjoyment. Closer analysis reveals that these are not as contradictory aims as they may seem. Sivananda Yoga cultivates highly committed disciples as the core of this group which in turn provide services to others, hoping that growing numbers of the latter will eventually become avid disciples as well.

The Rajneesh movement seems likewise to use retreats in distinctly different ways, both as a means of reinforcing the loyalty of committed members and as adventuresome, recreation for client-like participants interested for a short time in exploring their program of meditation exercises and therapies in open, experimental, congenial settings. As they filled out survey forms, Rajneesh followers living in Montreal acted as if Rajneesh centres were resources which they could draw upon as they chose in order to enhance their own sense of autonomy. In contrast, in person they stressed their devotion to Rajneesh as an exemplary prophet. Participants who are only temporary participants at Rajneesh centres are able to assert their independence while still recognizing a dependence upon Rajneesh both because they withdraw from the centre for periods of time and because Rajneesh for much of the time has remained a distant, non-demanding charismatic figure (Palmer and Bird, 1988).

One of the common features of the three groups surveyed was that participants idealized their leaders. Participants benefitted in part because leaders presented an attractive model of the kind of person they would like to be. The importance of leaders as ego ideals stands out when evaluations of leaders are compared with two other data, namely evaluations of parents as models and personal feelings of self-control. Respondents in all three groups overwhelmingly doubted they could significantly alter the course of their lives through pure will power. They were strongly inclined to view their own lives as being determined by impersonal forces over which they had no control (such as karma or the traits with which you were born) or the action of others (parents, people in power, the vicissitudes of fortune) (Table 7). Their sense of powerlessness was combined with a sense of personal confusion. Evidentially most respondents found it difficult to treat parents as exemplary models for their ego ideals (Table 5). In contrast leaders of these groups were regarded as being both able to effectively guide their own lives and do so with a sense of clarity and direction worth emulating. In other studies, it would be useful to examine more closely the variations in the role of leaders as therapists as this survey data does suggest that this relationship is central no matter what therapeutic approach is followed.

While in some new religious groups the relationship to the

group leader is viewed as being short term, in others it is viewed as long-lasting. Therapeutic activities take on different meanings depending on whether this relationship is viewed as terminable or interminable. Whenever participants act as devotees, worshippers or disciples, the relationship is on-going. Typically only an abbreviated range of therapeutic techniques are used, often primarily to reinforce communal commitments. Therapy assumes this function among core members of the Rajneesh group who subordinated their roles as clients of therapy to their roles as devotees and disciples of Rajneesh and his program of meditation and exercise. In contrast whenever participants act as clients, students, short term retreat-takers, their relationships to leaders and their groups are only short term. Respondents in both the TA and CA groups similarly viewed their relationships to their groups as terminable. Many people participated in the Rajneesh group with the similar assumption. Like most of the participants in new religious movements, their involvement was only for a short term.

NOTES

1. The research on which this paper is based was made possible in part by a research grant from the Ministry of Education of the Quebec government. We are grateful to the following persons who offered critical comments and helpful suggestions on earlier drafts of this paper: Laurence Nixon, Raymond Prince, James Richardson and Harvey Mann. An earlier version of this paper was presented at the Pacific Sociological Association Meetings (1983) at San Jose, California.
2. 60% of TA's especially valued these activities compared to 24% of the members of the Creative Awareness Group and none of the Rajneesh group.
3. The mean percentage of respondents who answered that their leader always or often accepted them was 80% and the percentage for TA participants was 86%. The mean percentage for respondents who answered that their leaders always or often made them feel closer to others was 38% and the percentage for TA participants was 43%.
4. 45% (mean average) of all respondents viewed their parents as being empathetic (extremely so and quite a lot); 42.5% of the religious respondents viewed their leaders as being equivalently empathetic; 80% of TA participants viewed their leader as empathetic.

5. Respondents must have meant before 1978, when Rajneesh became less publicly accessible or, at least, before 1982, when he ceased to speak. His books are basically spoken orations later transcribed from tapes.
6. Sannyasin members experience in these regards are no different than the experiences of persons who regularly participate in a number of yoga groups. Adherents of Sivananda Yoga, for example, regularly meditate and regularly attend weekend and week long retreats at one of several camps the group has established. But the Sannyasin group differs with regard to the relation of members to the leader.
7. 40% said they would avoid friends, if asked by the leader, 30% similarly stated that they would be willing to change their diet; and 20% indicated they would become celibate or allow Rajneesh to arrange their marriage.

5

THE MEANING OF DISCIPLESHIP: INTERVIEW WITH A RAJNEESH THERAPIST, SWAMI VEET ATITO
(Dr. Jack Rains)

(INTERVIEW CONDUCTED BY SUSAN J. PALMER)

This interview is in two parts which span a decade.

The first session took place in January, 1979, in his house in Montreal. Jack and I were teaching the same college, and when he returned from his summer vacation in India wearing orange, I asked him if I could interview him on his conversion experience. He actually interviewed himself, providing the tape recorder and speaking in a deep rich voice with a strong southern accent. I was not surprised to find out that he had had an earlier career as a radio announcer in Texas. He described his experiences vividly and illustrated them with anecdotes, so I left the house in a daze, feeling that I'd just had a free trip to Poona.

The second part of the interview took place in the symposium on May 20, 1989 when Jack responded to questions from the group on his relationship to his spiritual master and his work as a therapist.

Jack has a special role in the Montreal sannyasin community. He has never been a member of the commune, lives with his wife and son, and is around twenty years older than the "typical" thirtyish disciple. He is well-known among the local Rajneesh, however, because he regularly conducts therapy and meditation (Vipassana) workshops. Although he has a Ph.D. in psychology, he is involved in the more avant-garde techniques of psychotherapy which originated in the human potential movement.

INTERVIEW: PART ONE, January 1979 at Jack's house

Q: When I asked if I could interview you on your conversion to neo-sannyas you said it wasn't your first conversion.

A: Yes, I've had several conversions. I was raised a devout Catholic but began to break away from it in college. Part of it was studying psychology, reading Philip Wylie and part of it was that I began to get off on having a position against the church. It took time to feel I'd broken away—eating meat on Fridays was difficult; but eventually it was a relief to get that stuff out of my life.

Then after getting my PhD I started teaching at a college in Florida. By then I was a confirmed atheist. Belief in God seemed an empty proposition—rather like believing in a large invisible rock. I had a friend and colleague—Sam—and he and I used to spend a lot of time talking about religion. We got off on being atheists together.

So my first conversion happened around 1965. I picked up a book of Zen stories—do you know *Zen Flesh, Zen Bones*? It's an intriguing little book. There is something about those Zen koans that haunt you. You keep wondering what the point of that story was, and of course there isn't a point. But I didn't see them as connecting in any way with religion. Then I read Philip Kapleau's *The Five Pillars of Zen* and it began to recall Christianity. There was a story about a Zen master who on hearing a quote from the Bible said, "The person who said that was enlightened". When I read that I thought "So this is what religion is really about! Oh! so Jesus was an enlightened master! Churches have nothing to do with it." And in Kapleau's book at the end there are some case histories of people who've experienced *satori*—just ordinary people, American housewives and so on—and for the first time I began to realize that enlightenment was something real—and it might be a possibility for me. Then I met Philip Kapleau and he showed me how to sit—so it was the combination of what I was reading and thinking about, all that was a prelude to my conversion. Bhagwan talks about it in terms of heating water. Water can be boiling at 99 degrees and still be water and then—suddenly it's steam. If I had been able to look forward and see

The Meaning of Discipleship

the person I would become, I would have said that that person is mad. But if I look back to the person I used to be, I would say that that person was asleep.

Q: How long were you involved in Zen?

A: I had been practising Zen for about five years and had been going to the Rochester centre—I'd go up from Montreal on weekends ... and I was beginning to accumulate a lot of guilt. I began to notice this—that I would feel guilty about not sitting often enough or long enough or for not witnessing my life with enough intensity. And the Zen Centre began to bug me a bit, it was getting very Japanese in style of food—and the last straw was when they asked me to wear robes in the sitting room. I really felt I didn't want to put out $22.00 just so I could sit there when my ordinary clothes would do just as well. And there was something else going on in my life at the same time ... this is more to do with conversion ... it was to do with Catholicism. This is going to sound nuts ... It was like I'd been hammering on the doors of the church and screaming God and I hadn't been getting any answers. I was beginning to feel really bad.

Q: What exactly happened?

A: Nothing exactly happened, it's just that nothing was happening, nothing. I felt completely empty, as if I was in a void. I used to cry a lot and feel that life was meaningless, that here I was devoting myself to something and not getting anywhere. What I wound up doing ... I thought, "This much guilt from Zen I could get from Catholicism. Catholicism is as much as a path as anything is—anything is a path! So, I could be a Catholic if I really want to be something. And at least I would have a place to *put* my guilt—in confession!"

So I went back to the church. First I looked for a spiritual advisor—and was never able to find anyone high enough. So I went to the yellow pages and picked out a church and said "Whatever happens, Thy will be done." It meant that in order to do the sacraments I had to do a lot of stuff. My wife and I had to get married again in the church ... I had to do all that and I got myself completely straight with the Catholic church and then one morning it left me like ... it just disappeared.

I was in church one morning. I went to early mass at seven o'clock every morning for a year. I was completely faithful and rather into it in a way. I particularly enjoyed weekday masses when no one was there. But I'd been reading Krishnamurti and he really made me question the whole issue of believing in somethin again. Then my son was born and the problem of whether he was going to be baptised came up ... and one early morning mass ... it was on Christmas Eve ... it was a beautiful morning, it was snowing and the sun was shining and we were all huddled together in this dark church and I just suddenly knew there was as much God outside as inside, perhaps a little more. And I knew the priest well enough to know where he was at ... he didn't really believe in what he was doing. I looked up when he raised the host and at that moment I saw that it was just a piece of bread!

And then I was sort of masterless for a while. I hung out with some Krishnamurti—you can't call them followers, because Krishnamurti doesn't have followers, there's this little group of Krishnamurti—ites that meet and play his tapes and I got in on the fringes and then pulled back out. I wasn't doing meditations but I was still trying to stay conscious—Krishnamurti is funny about that—he sort of tells you that nothing can be done. He's a lovely man, undoubtedly enlightened—but he's not very helpful. People wind up listening to his tapes and doing nothing to transform themselves or their lives because he says there is nothing to do. And it's true from where *he* stands, but not from this side.

When I find someone like Krishnamurti I end up buying all their books and go through them one after another and end up squeezing the lemon dry. The surprises aren't happening anymore—you are familiar with their form of thought. So for a while I was just drifting along happy enough with life. I thought—"If this is all there is—it's good—it's enough."

Then I heard from my old friend Sam. He'd heard about Bhagwan through his dentist. He sent me a book by Bhagwan—and I sort of fell in love with him. This book contains six passages describing the moment of enlightenment—and I became totally convinced that whoever had written that was enlightened.

I still wasn't thinking of becoming a *sannyasin*, although I wanted closer contact with Bhagwan. But there were some things that put me a bit off him. He seems to accept a lot of pseudo scientific nonsense as being just the way it is—and I can't abide that. But he was so different from Krishnamurti. Krishnamurti is detached, cool, severe, and Bhagwan is playful, warm, he laughs a lot—and you never get the feeling that Krishnamurti ever laughs!

Q: So how did you become a *sannyasin*?

A: Well, I was doing a bit of therapy—counselling—on the side and had saved about $2,000.00 and was planning to revamp my hi-fi system. I phoned Sam and told him I was coming to New York to buy a new turntable and so on and he said "You're crazy! Why don't you go to Poona instead?" I'd never thought I could do that. It meant leaving Patience with our son. I've always been over—scrupulous about laying my trip on other people—I've never been out to covert people to Bhagwan and I didn't want Patience to have to make sacrifices for my religious trip, but in fact she was amenable to the idea. She thought if that was what I wanted to do I should certainly do it and, well, it was what I wanted to do. As Sam put it, "Why buy a hi-fi set when Jesus is waiting?"

So once I'd made the decision I left right away intending to take *sannyas* as soon as I got there. I didn't want to sit around testing the water. Just do it and get it over—but particularly because I wanted to come close to him. I had the sense that, though what Krishnamurti says is true—you don't have to have a master—it's certainly a lot easier. Also I kind of liked the *schtick* that goes with it—the orange clothes, the *mala*, the change of name. As I see it, it's a way of working of myself—to dress in orange—to make myself ridiculous in a certain way—and that's good for me.

Q: Is that what being a sannyasin involves?

A: Yes, it's like a game. Bhagwan calls it "the mad game"—master and disciple, a game you play when power and money no longer attract you. The orange signifies that you are a seeker—you are moving in an inner instead of an outer direction. These three things—the orange, the *mala*, the name, are the rules of this ridiculous game this man asks me to play in order to come near him.

Q: Can you describe what it was like to arrive in Poona—you know, your first impression and so on?

A: Well, the airplane arrives at Bombay and then you have this harrowing taxi ride to Poona—it's just awful, it's so scary! The taxi driver is trying to make time and the road is winding up a mountain and you're going past goats, chickens and cows and people everywhere on the road and there are huge trucks that are turned over—we saw seven trucks lying on their side and the driver would turn around and signal how many people had died in that one—so what do you do? You surrender! But you think, "I would at least like to see Bhagwan before I go."

Then I got into the Blue Diamond Hotel, the best in Poona, which is not saying much and went out to find the ashram.

My first impression was—I was dazed. First of all I had jet lag, then it was so green! It's like a green jungle inside the ashram and outside it's so dry and hard. There were guards around and I wasn't sure what I felt about that—they're there to keep order and to keep out dogs, children and beggars. As you enter the ashram there's a walkway that goes down towards "Buddha Hall" and there's lots of greenery on either side and up above. It's a very attractive place and the first day or two I just sat there and watched the people walk up and down and the energy flow between them. Someone would come along and smile at someone else, there's a lot of eye contact there—your eyes will come to rest on some one else even if you don't know the person and might rest in their gaze for a long time before anyone looks away. At any rate there was a lot of energy being transferred this way—that's how I saw it. You know some one would smile at some one else, or embrace and then they would leave and pass it on to someone else and you could see a whole microcosm—what Bhagwan calls the "Buddhafield". I began to feel very happy and joyous. I started doing a group there...

Q: A group?

A: They have eighty or ninety different groups—a bit like encounter groups. *Satori* was the name of my group. The way they are arranged is, they advise you to write a letter to Bhagwan saying "Here I am, I'm forty-seven years old, I teach psychology and I'm into Zen", and he writes back and gives you four groups and that takes care of your stay.

Q: How long did you stay there?

A: I intended to stay a month and ended up staying six weeks. On the tenth of the month everything changed over. He speaks English one month then Hindi one month and so on—and then for ten days after that there are no groups, just various meditations happening about the place. You can go to *Dynamic Meditation* at six, *Discourse* at eight, and after Discourse there's Sufi dancing. Then there's—Vipassana—. Also they play tapes in the afternoon. People sit around and rest, and then there's *Nadhabrahma*—a humming meditation. It sounds like a hive of bees. Each person hums on the outbreath. You do fifteen minutes of that and then ten minutes of this hand motion (he demonstrates). It's basically like this only done at half speed. Then you do up to ten minutes of *this* hand motion. Then you flake out for ten minutes.

Q: What does it mean, the hand motion? It seems to suggest a sort of emptying and filling of the self.

A: They don't explain anything that way. *Nadhabrahma*—that's about four in the afternoon and then after that is the music group. People dance together and sing all kinds of songs—repetitive type of songs that go for a long time. Everyone dances very freely and lots of people come to that because it is great fun. And then there comes the time . . . .

You see, he—is now holding *Darshan* somewhere in the ashram and ... this always sounds weird—he has a foot pedal which turns off all the lights in the ashram, so no matter where you are all the lights go out and you stop whatever you are doing and just sit quietly until they go back on. The idea is that everyone in the ashram is receiving his energy wherever they are.

I had arrived on June first and intended to leave on July first. I spent the first ten days sitting through lectures in Hindi and going to the meditations, and then I had my first group, *Wu wei* which lasted three days—it means "action in inaction" and you learned to allow the energy to move up your body. None of this was rationalized for you but the aim seemed to be to develop a witnessing consciousness. You sit opposite someone and they tell you what you are doing. There was a lot of interaction between people in that group and it was done mostly in the nude, which was a big surprise to me! I didn't know about this but the first thing the instructor said was, "Look, there'll be no nudity on the balcony or in the halls. Indians don't understand"—so everybody took off their clothes. This would have been a big hurdle for me if I'd known about it beforehand. But it turned out not to be such a big deal. At first everybody stands around and looks at everybody else, and then you realize that other people aren't so beautiful.

So there was that group and then I did *Enlightenment Intensive*. This was three day intensive group, with no talking or contact with anybody outside the group—no eye contact, body contact and living completely inside the ashram. Basically it was the koan "Who am I?" You sit opposite someone on a cushion and say, "Tell me who you are?" You have five minutes. You say, "Well, I'm ... so and so." They listen, don't judge—then you change over. You say, "Tell me who you are?" Then it changes back and changes back and then you change partners. This goes on for three days.

Q: What did you say about yourself?

A: At first I went through the stories about myself then when ran out I was forced to talk about who I was at that moment. At the end I would just sit silently looking at my partner.

The next group was *Rebirth*. You lie down on your back in a circle and everybody's heads are together in the middle of the room. There are three or four group leaders—they are called rebirthers—wandering among the heads telling you how to breathe. You increase the depth of breath that you pull in and let the exhaled breath just fall out of you. You keep increasing the depth and frequency. I didn't know what to expect. I thought it was just a breathing technique, but the usual thing that happens is, suddenly all your muscles are blocked and your hands and your feet get tightened up and you can't move.

Then the energy starts moving and I would feel it moving up my legs, then up my arms, then I could feel it up here, then in my throat where it stuck. I was gasping and really in bad shape. The rebirther was cradling my head and said "Keep breathing". She was so soft and beautiful—of course I couldn't *see* her, because I had to keep my eyes closed—but she was massaging my throat, and pulling me up—then I felt it all moving up through my head and then it all passed out through the top of my head. It was beautiful! I could feel my skin and there was nothing inside the skin—just the surface and the inside was completely empty. I felt terribly sensitive and vulnerable. There was a gnat that was playing around and I would feel its wings on my face.

But the experience surprised the hell out of me! By the time I realized what was happening it was too late to stop. It was like being on a roller coaster—to stop it midway would have been worse than to carry on through. I just had to put my trust in the fact that it was Bhagwan doing this—and he must know what he's doing...So there were three times of doing rebirth. The second time I was having a tremendous battle with my mind saying, "You did it yesterday and it was fantastic—but don't expect it to be the same today!" It got started and my mind said, "You've had it—it was pretty good—now let it go." There was this Japanese guy who was the rebirther and he kept encouraging me to continue and I really didn't want to. I was sort of scared—but I did it anyway.

It was like moving against my mind. My whole body was soaked with perspiration. The third time the experience was more peaceful and when I came out the whole world was transformed. It had just been raining and the colours were so brilliant, the sounds so clear!

We did this for three days. The actual rebirthing only took about twenty minutes, but we did other things. One afternoon we took turns lying in foetal position while people covered you in cushions. Then you would push against them and try to fight your way out while they would hold you in. Right after rebirthing you would sit down with paper and crayons and draw. There was a twelve year old girl there whose drawings were really beautiful.

The next meditation was *Vipassana*, but it was the first of July and I had agreed with Patience to stay only one month, so I went to the office to arrange my leave. The woman there, Lakshmi, said "Oh, but you must stay until the tenth! It says here that you are staying until the tenth." I explained that I had to be back and so on—but she said, "I understand, Swami wants you to stay for Gurupurnima Day!" This is a big festival day of all the gurus in India. I pointed out that my passport expires before then, and my flight date was set, but she said "Oh, that's no problem", and sent out a note to one of their doctors to write a letter saying I was sick and needed an extension. I wrote to Patience but received no answer and was worried—but it was clear I was meant to be there. Finally I phoned her and she'd just written back saying it was fine with her if I staying on an extra ten days.

So then I did a nine day group, *Vipassana*, which is seven hours a day of following the breath, interspersed with a half hour of walking slowly with the attention focused on the soles of the feet.

Q: Can you describe what you feel like when you meditate?

A: Well, obviously it changes. When I first started sitting it was freaky for me. Basically my practise in Zen was following my breath. I would feel great resistance to starting. Then I would go into it and my mind was going nuts and taking me with it. I went through this period—I think everyone goes through it—where you have a thought and think "I shouldn't be thinking" and then "I shouldn't be thinking I shouldn't be thinking".

The Meaning of Discipleship

Somebody finally clarified that for me. I was seeing it as a piling up of thoughts—each successive thought was stacked up on top of the last one—you know, here I am thinking a thought and here I am thinking about thinking a thought—but he pointed out that it was just a succession of thoughts.

You ask me how I felt. At the beginning that was what was going on. It's changed a lot over the years. At Poona doing *Vipassana* part of the time I felt I was going nuts—crazy. The main thing it did was broke my identity with my thoughts. They would drift by and you just weren't involved in them—there's the mind doing its thing. One thing that happened—we were just finishing lunch and my back hurts, so I stretch like this—and hit some girl on the nose. I of course turned to her and said "I'm sorry, are you all right?" which of course breaks the rule of silence. She didn't break the rule. She didn't look at me, just rubbed her nose and went back to her sitting place. He mat was next to mine and I'm thinking, "You bitch, you couldn't even make it alright—you're so miss goody two shoes!" My mind is just going like that. Then I wasn't involved with it and found it even kind of amusing. It went on for two hours. It was very strong at first and I identified strongly but then it was all gone. It was interesting to watch and find out how mechanical it all was. That's one thing I found out—my mind is *totally* mechanical.

For example, here there's thirty-one people in the group. They serve lunch on thirty-one identical plates, a dish of yogurt, one banana, rice and vegetables—and everyone is looking over the trays, myself included, to see which is the best one—but of course they are all the same. You see how petty and small the mind is and how utterly mechanical. You push one button and one thing comes up—you punch another...

Q: Then what is left, if you are not the mind?

A: Well, *I* was still there. There is only awareness. The mind does all the thinking, but *it* was just there and I am it. It's not something you can verbalize like "Here I am being the witness," because once you say that you are identifying with the thoughts. So I couldn't take possession of my awareness and say "yes, I've really reached it". But there is just the awareness and there are thoughts, these body feelings, sounds from the outside all like a screen surrounding you, like a film of life.

Q: Was it a blissful feeling?

A: I had a couple of really serene hours, wonderful moments—but I wasn't in bliss as I understand it. I wasn't in *samadhi*. My thoughts were still there. So out of nine days I had two perfect hours and then there were two hours of hell, absolute torture!

Q: Why?

A: Oh, I felt like my bottom was churning—all the energy inside me and my thoughts were going a mile a minute. I took it to the group leader. "Every fibre of my being wants to split and I know I'm not going to which doesn't make it any better, and it's chaos inside, absolute chaos!"
The group leader said, "That's right, that's good, just watch it!"

Q: Can you tell me about how you were initiated into sannyas? Was it a special ritual?

A: Now when you take *sannyas* you go to a Darshan. What happens is you are called, and you come up and sit in front of Bhagwan and he says "Close you eyes" and he writes out your name on a piece of paper in regular letters and in sanskrit, signs it, dates it and then he says "Open your eyes and come closer" and he takes a *mala* and hangs it around your neck and puts his thumb in the middle of your forehead and looks deeply into your eyes, and then sits back and says, "Your name is Swami Veet Atito which means `beyond the past'", and then he began to talk about western psychology. He talked about Freud and Jung in connection with being preoccupied with the past, and for a *sanyassin* the past is behind them.
I couldn't understand how to take it. You see, the kind of psychology I'm into, phenomenology, is precisely beyond the past. So is he telling me to drop the past? Is he telling me who

I am or who I am going to be? If he thinks he's giving me directions in my involvement with psychology he's really wrong. He doesn't know what I'm into.

But there was one moment that pierced through all that—it was a shock for me. The night before the Darshan I had been walking along the road to my group and there was a gorgeous sunset and I stopped for I don't know how long to watch it and then went on. But when he was talking about being beyond the past he said "For example, you are walking along and suddenly there's a sunset and the mind stops and you are with the sunset and then you move on". My mind was thinking "He's got spies. How does he know this?" Then I said, "You're being silly, it's just a coincidence. Then the other part even figured out who it was because I remembered when I turned around there was a girl I knew who was sitting there—"Aha, she's got an inner line to Bhagwan!" For she was one of the older ones—she's been there for five or six years but not one of the "power ladies" as we call them who run the ashram. Anyways that's what was going though. It shocked me and I didn't know how to take it.

When I attended my *Leaving Darshan*, I was given a small wooden box with something of Bhagwan in it—a hair, or nail clipping, I don't know what because you are supposed to never open it. See, it's over there on my shelf.

Q: How do you see your relationship with Bhagwan Rajneesh?

A: Well, in the old days before three years ago—there used to be a lot more contact with him—there were a lot less people around him. Now there is less of a feeling that he knows who you are. Or maybe he knows who you are in a way you don't know who you are.

My friend, Sam, was frustrated by this. He found Bhagwan somewhat distant, perfunctory in his attitude. Everyone goes there hoping to be noticed, of course, wanting to be close to Bhagwan. So what Sam did was to write down all the Jewish jokes he knew and sent them to Bhagwan. When he went to his *Leaving Darshan*, he found Bhagwan still ignored him—but he used four of his jokes! So in a way it was a kind of communication.

When I was there he was good to me. I wrote him a letter after my first group describing it and how it had affected me and I said that at last I felt "home"—that I somehow belonged there. The next day I got a note which said "See Arup" and she told me that Bhagwan had asked her to ask me to stay!

Q: What is a Leaving Darshan?

A: Basically the newcomers attend three *Darshans* during their stay—the *Arrival Darshan*, the *Leaving Darshan* and the *Sannyas Darshan*. There is also an *Energy Darshan* in which a group of "power ladies" surround the person and hold his hands and Bhagwan presses his forehead. I could have ordered one through Arup, but I didn't think of it. There is a Darshan every evening, but only one or two hundred people attend it, as opposed to the one thousand or more who attend the morning Discourse. It used to be more intimate but right now things are really booming there.

Q: What kind of relationship did you have with the people at Poona?

A: Well, I met one man who ran a fast food chain in Southern California. He was an ex-alcoholic. We sort of became friends and both had this sense of being on a roller-coaster where you are changing in spite of yourself, and changing in other ways than you intended. I met some other people, including an old friend who teaches at Rutgers who turned out to be one of the older sannyasins. On the whole I'd say my relationship with the people there was simpler—there was a whole lot less nonsense than there usually is in relating to people, and less attachment. I could be with people and that was nice, or I could be alone and that was nice.

I know I have changed from what other people tell me. I am more open to people—and more willing to express my negative feelings. I used to pretend not to be angry, but now I show it. I feel more open and vulnerable and my relationship with the world is much clearer. There is less ego concern. I used to be more concerned about appearing bright and interesting. I tend to trust my own perceptions more so that if I'm criticised I don't worry, and praise doesn't necessarily make me high.

Q: How has being a sannyasin affected your life here? Are you involved with the Rajneesh Meditation Centre?

A: No, I've been there but I find their schedule inconvenient and prefer a more solitary type of meditation. My practise now consists of witnessing, of being aware of what I'm doing when I'm doing it. For example when I'm sitting on the metro I let my eyes move around. One moment they will be attracted to the bright orange of a woman's coat lining. Then they will move on to something else—and I watch my mind. I put my attention in my belly and feel each moment. I will get distracted, and then the attention comes back.

PART TWO: *May 20th 1989 at the Symposium on the Rajneesh Movement*

Q: Could you tell us about the meaning of discipleship?

A: Well, what do you do with a spiritual master? You surrender. It seems to me that everybody who was about to surrender—had something that was a sticking point for them, like, "Oh, he drives a Rolls Royce. I can't stand that!" Some others would say, "He has asthma. How can he be enlightened if he has asthma? Everyone knows that if you're enlightened you can't get asthma or back pains". I have a friend who is a mathematician, and every time Bhagwan started to talk about mathematics, he would squirm! For me, he gets kind of space cadet-like every now and then and he starts to talk about, oh, how plants can feel your thoughts—things like that for me were an extraordinarily iffy business. I am trained as a experimental psychologist and it sounds alot like bullshit to me ... So every time Bhagwan would talk like this, *I* would squirm—my friend the mathematician, it was no problem for *him*—and that was a sticking point for me, and I think that unless there *is* a sticking point and you can let go and say "OK, Bhagwan, you can have that one"—then you can't truly surrender.

For me it happened when someone asked Bhagwan, "Why are Jews so smart? In the last century we've had Marx, Freud, Einstein—all brilliant men who've changed our world, so why are Jews so smart?" And Bhagwan said, "Well, after the Jewish boy is born"—he had the date wrong, 5 or 6 days, "the foreskin is cut off and all the energy from the foreskin goes directly to the brain—and that's why Jews are so smart." And once I heard that, I just gave up!

So it's about surrender—Bhagwan was always very careful about that—and he says, "You're not to follow me—I don't have followers—I have lovers, I have friends. You are not to imitate me, all I want is for you to become yourself. Be like you!" ... so a good part of discipleship is getting over my own barriers to becoming myself.

The next thing about being a disciple is ... when something happens that isn't supposed to, or something terrible happens in your life, the question is, how do I learn from that?

So that when the Ranch collapsed and ..."the bubble burst", that was the question. This was something unusual, and I *hated* it. I hated it! The whole business. The publicity, Bhagwan trying to escape in a plane, it looked like he was lying on television— I hated that. But then after a while I began to realise that something really wonderful had happened. It was as if he had taken a whole bunch of people and sort of twisted them around— like this—and then Woop! he sends them flying off in all directions. I began to see what a wonderful thing he had done. It was painful, but I learned more from that than I could have learned any other way!

Q: How has being a disciple of Rajneesh affected your work as a therapist?

A: First of all, I think that in therapy if one has a technique and everyone that comes to you—you do the same technique—it's like fixing a television set—give them a tweak here and tweak there—I think it's an incredibly boring life! No matter how effective you are, you're not growing.

To me, one of the things that being a Rajneeshee has changed

The Meaning of Discipleship

in my own therapy is that I'm a *lot* more spontaneous! I know one wonderful success story—you'll like this. I wish I had done this but it happened to a friend of mine ...

He had a woman who came to him and she couldn't stop throwing up, like she'd been throwing up for seven or eight years. She'd been in psychoanalysis for five years and she always carried barf bags in her purse and Kleenex.

Nothing touched this problem. She went to see this Rajneesh therapist—the first visit—and of course she had these airsick bags with her and she opened one and set it down here and she had her Kleenex here and she would be talking about her problem and she'd say, "Excuse me a moment" and she'd throw up and she'd put the bag back down—And she was *very* elegantly dressed, perfectly coiffed, absolutely immaculate ... and never got a drop of her.

So what my friend did—without even thinking apparently, he just reached over and grabbed the bag and threw it all over her! Like this! That finished the problem! She's so grateful to him. To this day she's very grateful to him. One session—amazing!

It's that spontaneity that works. If he'd taken a few minutes to think—wait a minute, should I do that or not? Instead he just acted on a kind of immediate intuition which he couldn't explain. Nobody knows why that worked, but it worked.

And for me, that's what's interesting in being a therapist. I found that, through what I did at the Ranch and in groups—I was able to trust intuition rather than some formula. For me, it's not interesting to do things by a set of rules. What is interesting is to get into a real close relationship with this person and then see what happens—just happens!

6

RAJNEESH WOMEN: LOVERS AND LEADERS IN A UTOPIAN COMMUNE

Susan J. Palmer

New religious movements (NRMs) have been a focus of interest for sociologists for over a decade. Nevertheless, in contrast to the depth of interest in women's roles in nineteenth century American utopias (Kern, 1981; Foster, 1981; Hansen, 1981), the experiments with sex roles and marriage patterns occurring in some of the contemporary spiritual communes have received little serious attention. In recent years scholars have begun to include gender-related issues in their studies of NRMs (Rochford, 1981), but, aside from a few accounts of fundamentalist Christian communes (Richardson et al., 1979; Wallis, 1984; Pfaffenberger, 1982) and an in-depth study of Unificationist sexuality (Grace, 1985), the alternative patterns of family life developing in communal NRMs remain largely undocumented.

The Rajneesh movement has only recently become the object of scholarly interest (Carter, 1987; Gordon, 1987), although it received extensive media coverage in the 1980's due to the legal battles and land use disputes surrounding the movement's attempt to build a utopian city in Oregon (*Oregonian*, 1985; Fitzgerald, 1986). There has been, however, no serious attempt to document and analyze the alternative sex roles or patterns of sexuality in the Rajneesh communes which, between 1981 and 1985, were as distinctive, as highly evolved, and as different from the larger society, as those of the Shakers, the Oneida community and the Mormons in the nineteenth century. Aside from salacious descriptions of nudity and violence in the therapy groups in Poona in the late 1970's by Christian anti-cultists (Van Leen, 1980), and glowing descriptions of the "free love" society at Rajneeshpuram by journalists who evidently found the utopian atmosphere contagious (Braun, 1984; *Penthouse*, July 1985), this aspect of the movement has largely been ignored.

There is a striking diversity in the roles available to women in communal style NRMs. As was noted in a previous paper, sex roles tend to be more clearly defined in these groups than in the larger society, and this clarity is often achieved by emphasizing one role and de-emphasizing or rejecting other roles (Palmer, 1988). For example, female devotees of Krishna are "mothers" by title and occupation, but they can never be friends or lovers in relation to the males. Women in the Unification Church begin their careers as celibate "sisters" and become the "daughters" of Reverend Moon when he blesses them in marriage to one of their "brothers". Thus Unificationist women enjoy a wider range of roles, but in a sequence which involves many levels of purification and initiation. The role of "lover", however, is proscribed (Grace, 1985).

Rajneesh women conform closely to this pattern in that they reject the roles of wife and mother and assume the role of "lover." This role not only has a high cultural value within the movement, but is considered to be a valid spiritual path. Although many Rajneeshee are involved in long-term relationships (particularly the older members and leaders), the most prevalent pattern in the Rajneesh communes is for men and women to engage in short term, pluralistic, heterosexual relationships. Since this pattern is unusual among NRMs (particularly the "oriental imports" which tend to arrange marriages or promote celibacy), and since a certain stigma is attached to sexually promiscuous women in the larger society, the central question in this study will be the following: Why do women choose to live in the Rajneesh communes which demand the renunciation of motherhood and marriage and offer a style of living which could be described as a never-ending series of short-lived, intense, and overlapping love affairs?

In the course of researching this NRM, certain facts and findings emerged which appear relevant to this question. Rajneesh women are considerably older than women in ISKCON and the Unification Church (around thirty-five to forty), and are more likely to be recruited from the upper and upper-middle classes and to have received graduate degrees. Many of the women interviewed for this study had achieved success in their professional life before joining the Rajneesh movement, a characteristic which corresponds with the findings of Carter (1987) and Braun (1984). A second clue to this NRM's appeal for women can be found in the discourses of Rajneesh in which he exalts women over men and paints utopian visions of a new age based on a radical restructuring of relations between the sexes. He provides glimpses of a new spiritually liberated woman, a female Buddha who is physically beautiful and sexually expressive, who will rule in the new millennium after two-thirds of the world's population has been decimated by AIDS, and who will build a society characterized by ecological harmony, technological advancement and meditative consciousness. Thirdly, on the basis of the interview data, it appears that one of the main attractions of this group lies in Rajneesh's philosophy of sexuality. Several sannyasins who had encountered Rajneesh while on the "guru circuit" in India, noted that he was unique among gurus in that he does not "put down" women or advocate celibacy but, on the contrary, insists that sex is the path to enlightenment.

In view of this and other findings I will attempt to prove the following hypothesis: that this movement attracts a particular type of woman, the middle-aged, upper-middle class woman who is accustomed to independence and a lucrative employment, and who tends to be childless, unmarried, and highly educated. Moreover, one reason why these women choose to participate in this particular NRM is because it offers an alternative philosophy of sexuality which is consistent with their previous lifestyle, and which validates their life choices. Finally, it will be argued on the basis of data found in the interviews that the role of "lover" in the Rajneesh Foundation International (RFI) is perceived by these women as offering *religious* solutions to problems of intimacy and family life encountered in the larger society. In order to present a coherent picture of Rajneeshee sexuality and to attempt to prove my argument, the following strategy will be adopted:

1) Rajneesh's philosophy of sexuality will be presented.
2) Sex roles and sexual relationships in the Rajneesh com-

munes will be described.
3) Available data on the membership will be cited.
4) The changes in the patterns of family life since World War II will be examined, according to the theories of Glendon (1985) and Berger and Kellner (1974), focusing on how these changes have affected the roles and life-styles of women. The ways in which Rajneesh "family" patterns represent extreme responses to, or parodies of, these changes will be demonstrated.
5) Five reasons for this movement's appeal for women will be proposed, as religious "solutions" to the confusion and dilemmas arising from changing patterns of sexuality in the larger society.

Rajneesh's Philosophy of Sexuality

Rajneesh's ideas on sex roles and sexuality can be found throughout his discourses and, in a concentrated form, in *The Book* (1984), which is a codification of his thought listed in alphabetical order. Recently, *A New Vision of Women's Liberation* (1987) presents a coherent picture of his philosophy of sexuality, the main components of which can be summed up as follows:

a) He equates sexual feelings with meditative states of consciousness, and recommends exploring one's sexuality as a spiritual path leading to enlightenment, the "cosmic orgasm":

Meditation is a by-product of orgasmic experience.... What happens? Time stops, thinking disappears.... To be exactly true, meditation is a non-sexual orgasm (NVWL:28).

b) He states that people are naturally polygamous and that women have more sexual "energy" than men, and, hence, are spiritually more evolved:

Women are capable of multiple orgasms, man is not. Sexually man is very poor compared to woman. ...[S]he has not even started and you are finished—that is very embarrassing. Because of this fear man has repressed women all over the world (The Book, on "Woman").

c) He advocates "free love," calling marriage "the coffin of the love" (*The Rajneesh Bible*, 1985). He views marriage as man's attempt to own and control women, and also as the cowardly attempt to cling to love which is, as he sees it, essentially ephemeral and changing.

d) He emphasizes the individual's autonomy and the necessity for non-attachment and solitude on the spiritual path. He claims that women are more self-sufficient and independent than men.

e) He recommends living in communes and renouncing the family:

The biological family must be destroyed. Only the spiritual family will remain. (The Sound of Running Water, 1978).

f) He discourages parenthood and pregnancy for three reasons: because of the overpopulation of the planet, because it degrades woman to a baby factory, and because it interferes with individual self-development. He approves of test tube babies as a method of eugenics for the future:

The scientific thing would be for every hospital to have a sperm bank...and a couple can have an absolutely definite choice about what kind of child they want...and the sperm should be provided by the hospital and injected into the woman, so from the very beginning the idea of possessiveness is cut. ...[T]his is getting out of the imprisonment of biology.... The father is unknown and the mother has only provided her womb; the child belongs to the commune...possessiveness is out of the question...within a few years...eggs from the mother can also have a bank in the hospital, and the womb can be mechanical. It will look inhuman at the beginning but it will create a far better society (NVWL: 1987:86).

As the passages above illustrate, Rajneesh has developed a philosophy of sexuality which is quite as radical and elaborate as those of Ann Lee, Joseph Smith and John Humphrey Noyes. The latter's ideas on "philopropogativeness" resemble Rajneesh's notions of parenthood expressed above. Moreover, like these millenarian prophets of the past, and Reverend Sun Myung Moon today, his ideas on sexuality are inextricably bound up with his new millennium:

> My own vision is that the coming age will be the age of woman. Man has tried for five thousand years and failed.... It is enough! Now feminine energies have to be released.
> And unless women become enlightened they cannot be really free because enlightenment is the ultimate in freedom. The freedom of women cannot come through stupid movements like Women's Liberation.... If we can create a few woman Buddhas in the world then woman will be freed from all chains and fetters.... Love is going to be her meditation...that is going to be her path towards light, towards godliness. And out of love woman will have a new birth. She will become a child of light, a child of moonlight.... And you can see that thousands of women are gathered around me. It has never happened before. It has always been a male-dominated quest (*The Book*, on "Woman").

Sex Roles and Sexual Relationships in the Communes

Before attempting to describe Rajneeshee sex roles and sexual mores, it is important to note the following impediments to accuracy and clarity. First, Rajneesh often contradicts his own statements and this could have some bearing on the fact that different sannyasins express widely different interpretations of what "Bhagwan says." Secondly, patterns of family life have changed throughout the course of the movement. They were at their most extreme during the Rajneeshpuram era (1981 to 1985), but since the communes have disbanded are becoming less "deviant," more "mainstream". Finally, although the international communes were modelled on Rajneeshpuram, they were by no means identical in their patterns of sexuality and leadership to it, or to each other.

Leadership and Work Roles

True to Rajneesh's vision of women as "the pillars of my

temple," women dominated the leadership of the movement (except for Bhagwan "Himself"). Braun notes that women controlled over 80 percent of executive positions in Rajneeshpuram. In the Montreal Rajneesh commune in 1985, the work was divided into ten departments, or "temples": kitchen, construction, cooking, cleaning, reception, restaurant, secretary, graphics, and accounting. Eight of the department heads were women. Both communes made a self-conscious effort to abolish sex divisions in work roles. Rajneeshpuram women were conspicuous in their operation of heavy earth moving equipment used in the massive construction program. *Penthouse* admiringly describes beautiful, scantily clad, teenage girls driving bulldozers, and the videocassette *The Way of the Heart* shows Maneesha directing the construction while wearing a hard hat and work boots. In Montreal, a swami ran the commune's daycare, and the directors of the commune were two women, Paras (1983-1985) and Khudai (1985-1986). Women and men worked side by side in a playful and flirtatious atmosphere. Female coordinators were called "moms," and in Rajneeshpuram the core group were referred to as the "supermoms." Swamis interviewed would explain the female leadership as a means to achieve true equality because "Bhagwan says woman are much more in touch with the heart, more receptive and grounded, less likely to get caught up in power trips."

Women in Ritual

Women played a dominant role in ritual and were considered to have superior charismatic qualities to men in that they were more receptive than men, and therefore a better receptacle for "Bhagwan's energy." Rajneesh was constantly accompanied by his core group of attractive women who surrounded his chair during the evening discourses. Belfrage (1984) describes the participation of Vivek, Maneesha, and Lakshmi during the initiation *darshans* in Poona. The women who danced around Rajneesh's chair as he sat enthroned during his silence, were called "mediums". The mediums performed the Energy *Darshans* and exhibited charismatic gifts: "[They] would whirl around filled with Bhagwan's energy and then they would touch us and zap!" A sannyasin claimed their function was "to transmit Bhagwan's *shakti* to his disciples." Former mediums claimed to have had sexual contact with Bhagwan for the purpose of "stimulating our lower chakras," for "rewiring my circuits," and for "orchestrating our energies" (Gordon, 1987:79).

Sexual Identity

Although Rajneesh emphasizes that men and women possess very different spiritual qualities, there was a tendency to undermine sexual distinctions in the Montreal commune. This was evident in the unisex look in clothing and in the living arrangements. In Poona women and men both wore loose shifts and waist-length hair (Gunther, 1979: photoessay). Once the group moved to America, members abandoned the hippie look, and men and women cut their hair short and wore loose elegant trousers and tank tops. When I first began to visit the Montreal commune, I was struck by the men's fashion for earrings and perfume and low-necked T shirts which, to the untutored eye, might be mistaken for the "gay look." Unlike the Unification Church and ISKCON, there was no segregation of the sexes in living arrangements. Bathrooms, bedrooms, and dining tables were shared by both sexes.

Commune life appeared to foster close friendships between the sexes. Men and women would confide in each other and receive advice and comfort concerning their love affairs. Men were physically affectionate with each other in a manner unusual in North American culture, and were constantly hugging, "roughhousing" and wrestling on the floor. It was not unusual to see a man sitting on another man's lap weeping and the other stroking his hair. Women embraced each other constantly and it was customary for women to sit facing each other, one on the other's lap with her legs locked around her waist in order to be rocked like a child, particularly after a "heavy" time in a therapy group.

Homosexuality, however, was not encouraged. Commune members claimed there were no homosexuals among them, except for a bisexual lesbian couple. Several members claimed that when the group moved to Oregon, Sheela had announced that all the homosexuals had to leave. However, homosexuality is not considered sinful or abominable (as in the UM or ISKCON), but rather as a cowardly "cop out." Teertha's response to a self-confessed lesbian in his therapy group was, "You are trying to hide from the terror of the unknown. Your own sex is a small puzzle, the opposite sex is a big puzzle."

Sexual Relationships

The Montreal commune could fairly be described as an ongoing sex therapy workshop in which short-term, pluralistic sexual relationships were the norm. This pattern was based on an ideal of communal sharing and equality in love, and on Rajneesh's emphasis on sexual expression. There were various control mechanisms in the group which reinforced and regulated this pattern of sexual behaviour. The Rajneesh therapy groups that aspiring initiates were obliged to participate in, employed various exercises and techniques which encouraged members to release inhibitions, express sexual feelings and learn new patterns of sexual relating. The ritual "hug" with which members frequently greeted each other and which they resorted to in order to refresh their spirits during their twelve-hour work days, encouraged physical intimacy among members, but was also understood as reinforcing their spiritual identity and revitalising their "connection to Bhagwan" whose "energy" was immanent in the community or *sangha*. Sexual feelings were interpreted as charismatic indications of Bhagwan's presence "flowing" between his disciples. It was common to see a man and woman seated opposite each other in the cafe holding each other's hand pressed against their chests with their eyes closed and breathing deeply. When I first inquired about this behaviour I was told they were "feeling the heart connection."

Although there was a strong pressure exerted by the community on the individual to behave in a way that would probably be considered sexually hyper-active and promiscuous in the larger society, there was also considerable evidence in the interviews that members enjoyed some degree of choice and autonomy in their private lives. For example, one of the female directors informed me that for her first year in the commune she had remained celibate. The other director had been with the same lover for seven years. I noticed that the older and more established members, particularly the leaders, seemed to be involved in long-term relationships.

This appeared to be the pattern also in Rajneeshpuram where many of the supermoms and therapists were married or lived with long-term lovers. On the other hand, exclusive sexual relationships were frowned upon. One swami outside the commune who admitted to being happily married for fifteen years added, "I couldn't stand being married to a woman who was faithful!" In the course of interviewing commune members, I received the impression that long-term lovers were *secretly* faithful to each other. It was a prevalent notion that "sharing energy" with others enriched one's love affair; that one's lover would lose interest and the "energy" would become "stuck" if one were too devoted and exclusive. For those suffering from jealousy, the recommended panacea was to find another lover, which might succeed in renewing one's original lover's interest. Judging from accounts in interviews and public confessions in therapy groups, the members' love lives appeared to be a never-ending struggle between maintaining a strong diadic relationship on one hand, and integrating it into a group which demanded communal sharing on the other.

Couples joining the movement or entering the commune almost invariably seemed to split up and find new lovers. Most recent members claimed to have been with many lovers the first year or two in the commune but eventually settled down with one person. Women, who outnumbered the men by a small margin and tended to be slightly older, were encouraged to be the sexual aggressors. One swami who had lived in Rajneeshpuram said, "It was pretty common to have a woman come up to you on the street and say, 'Look, I've seen you around the last couple of days and I find you very attractive'. And then you'd go off for coffee and probably end up in bed." It was not uncommon to see couples in the commune in which the woman was at least ten years older than the man; there was a conscious effort to abolish agist attitudes.

The Membership

If one compared the members of the Rajneesh movement to those of other communal-style NRMs (those groups most likely to develop alternative sex roles and patterns of family life), one finds that the Rajneeshee tend to be significantly older, and to have a larger proportion of female members.

There is considerable evidence that the average age of a Rajneeshee is between thirty-two and forty. Kirk Braun claims that in 1981 the mean age of Rajneeshpuram residents was thirty-seven (Braun, 1982:71-71). Fitzgerald cited a survey made by the University of Oregon's Department of Psychology, which found the average age of Rajneeshpuram residents to be thirty-four in 1985 (Fitzgerald, 1986:58). Carter notes that Rajneesh members do not fit into Levine's *rite de passage* theory of cult conversion (Levine, 1984) because:

> Rajneesh are almost uniformly older and at a later stage in their lives before turning to the movement and rather than chance recruitment by strangers as described by Levine (1984) sannyasins indicate an active pursuit of Rajneesh training after referral by friends. Some have been drawn by advertised therapies (Carter, 1987:164-165).

The following statistics on the members of the Montreal Grada Rajneesh commune when at its peak, in December 1985, were given to me by Khudai, the director:

Average Age	Women; 34:25	Men; 32:71
Number of Members	31	28
Youngest	22	24
Oldest	55	47

The Montreal residents are younger in mean age than the Rajneeshpuram residents (in their early as opposed to late thirties). This is perhaps explained by their attracting a high proportion of recent local converts, whereas Rajneeshpuram was established by the older (in terms of years of involvement) core group of disciples.

Rajneesh recruits tend to come from upper-middle to middle

class families. They conform closely to Donald Stone's typical participant in the Human Potential Movement who tends to be 35, single or divorced, and "never having had children" (Stone, 1976). Since the majority of Rajneeshee continue to live in the world after initiation, and tend to join at a later stage in their lives than the ISKCON devotees, they are far more likely to hold post graduate degrees or to have established themselves in their careers, as Fitzgerald and Braun have noted:

> ...eighty percent of the disciples came from middle-class or upper-middle-class backgrounds; their fathers were, overwhelmingly, professionals or businessmen. Some eighty-three percent of the Rajneeshee had attended college; two-thirds had bachelor degrees, and twelve percent had doctorates (Fitzgerald, 1986:58).

Carter's research project at Washington State University arrived at a similar conclusion concerning the social background of sannyasins:

> Initiates are almost uniformly drawn from the apparently successful, either aristocratic Europeans or accomplished professionals from Europe, the United States, Canada, Japan, India. Members include attorneys, physicians, writers, artists, academicians, and other professionals. Many sannyasins characterize themselves as the "dropouts" from the top of society and indicate disillusionment with bureaucratic institutions and industrial societies (Carter, 1987, *JSSR* 26:163).

Studies of the Krishna Consciousness movement have established that the majority of the recruits are white, upper-middle class males in their early to mid-twenties. Judah found that 85 percent of devotees were twenty-five or younger, and only 3 percent were over thirty (Judah, 1974:111).

The average age of Unificationists today is in the mid-to-late twenties according to studies conducted by Barker and Grace. Barker states, "The average age has remained fairly constantly around 23 years. In 1976 nearly 80 percent of the British membership was aged between 19 and 30; in 1978 the average (mean) age of full-time Moonies in both Britain and America was 26..." (Barker, 1985:206).

If one looks at the sex ratios of other well-known NRMs which have also established spiritual communes, it is evident that these movements have a greater appeal for men. The Unification movement in Britain and America has a sex ratio of 2:1 in favour of men, according to Barker's figures (Barker, 1985:206). She speculates on the reasons for this difference—the fact that women marry earlier than men, and the unsympathetic attitudes of the UM towards feminism—but concludes: "I have no clear explanation as to why more men than women are attracted to full-time membership" (Barker, 1985:206).

James Grace postulates that "the opening up of leadership positions for men might explain why there are considerably more male than female members in the movement" (Grace, 1985:104), and claims the ratio is 64 percent to 36 percent.

Of ISKCON, Johnson states that "In most regular temples men outnumber the women by about two to one" (Johnson, 1976:46). Rochford discovered that over one-half the members joined before their twenty-first birthday, and only one-fifth are unmarried, which suggests that the sex ratio at this phase of the movement was 3:2, since it is very rare to find unmarried females (aside from the *brahmacarinis*) in the movement (Rochford, 1985:46-47). The Children of God also evidently attract more men than women, since Wallis states that among the single members, men outnumber women by about 2:1 (Wallis, 1979).

Unlike these male-dominated NRMs, both numerically and structurally, the RFI attracts more female than male adherents. The ratio of women to men fluctuated during the different phases of the movement, and there are conflicting reports. It is clear, however, that women in the Poona ashram outnumbered the men. A photo-diary of Poona published by the RFI, *The Sound of Running Water* (1980), states, "Women outnumber the men three to one. In this way our group resembles the following of Buddha and Lao Tzu whose disciples were mainly women."

Hugh Milne's estimate is less dramatic. He writes:

> Of the thousand or so sannyasins at least six hundred were women, and nearly all were sexually active. All who come, female and male, had been attracted at least in part by a guru who advocated sexual experiment of the freest kind (Milne, 1986:134).

The discrepancy between these two ratios, 3:1 and 6:4, is probably accounted for if one assumes that the first estimate refers to the permanent residents of Poona, and the second includes the visitors. Neither account makes this clear, however.

Milne complains about the shortage of women in the Chidvilas ashram in New Jersey and during the first winter on the Ranch. But once Rajneeshpuram was established and began attracting visitors to its summer festivals, women again outnumbered men by a slight margin, according to former residents I interviewed. None of them, even a woman who had been in charge of statistics, could quote any exact figures, however.

Two long-term residents at Poona and Rajneeshpuram guessed that there were around 15 percent more women there. Montreal commune members sometimes commented on their fortunate situation in having almost an equal ratio—31:28 in favour of women.

The inevitable question which this sex ratio and portrait of members raises is: what is it about the Rajneesh movement which attracts women, and women of the single, childless, financially advantaged, middle-aged variety in particular? In order to answer this question it is important to look at studies of the dilemmas, social, emotional, and "romantic," which confront this class of women in America.

Rajneesh Women and Social Change

As the passages quoted from *A New Vision of Women's Liberation* indicate, Rajneesh has some interesting things to say about sexuality and spiritual life. In his discourses he presents visions of a new society based on woman's sexual, social, and spiritual liberation. His movement has fostered new attitudes towards sexual relationships and family life. Among the more striking attitudes and policies in the RFI which differentiate it from other movements are:

 a) the number of women in positions of authority
 b) the discouraging of exclusive couples and the rejection of marriage
 c) the fostering of immediate intimacy with no courting stage
 d) the ban on pregnancy and childbirth and the loosening of parent-child bonds.

The inevitable question arises: what does all this mean in terms of a) its significance for female adherents, b) as a response to or reflection of modern family life?

In order to answer this question it is necessary to step back and look at the changing patterns in families and sex roles during the past generation, as noted by Glendon (1985), Berger and Kellner (1974) and Bellah et al. (1985).

Cultural and Social Changes in Family Life

In the post-World War II period there have been dramatic changes in the patterns of family life and in the roles of women in industrialized societies of North America and Western Europe. The overall trends can be described as a move away from the set of assumptions basic to nuclear family patterns. These assumptions were the following:

> The basic family unit was a husband, wife and approximately two children living together without the likelihood of divorce.

> The husband was the primary breadwinner, the mother the housekeeper, and the children were raised at home.

Yankelovitch, in *New Rules* (1979), estimated that 70 percent of all American households conformed to this model in 1950. By 1981 only 15 percent did so.

As Glendon (1985) notes, the modern family departs from the traditional nuclear family in that it is no longer a single model, but represents a variety of coexisting types. For example, single person or parent households, cohabiting couples, married couples without children, reconstituted families, and double-income families have all become common non-nuclear patterns. In addition to these changes, more children are spending their pre-school years in day-care.

As a result of these changes, couples cannot simply fall into a well-established set of assumptions about family life. They must choose their own set of guidelines (Berger and Kellner, 1974). Bromley and Busching (1988) note the increased popularity of premarital agreements and handbooks offering helpful hints on formulating do-it-yourself style marriage contracts.

Larger cultural movements have undoubtedly had their effects on (or been affected by) the modern family. The woman's liberation movement with its emphasis on equal work, opportunity and pay; the gay movement; the sexual revolution with its emphasis on non-procreative sex; and finally, the increased emphasis on individual happiness and autonomy, are outstanding examples.

These changes have taken their emotional toll on individuals, and have created considerable confusion concerning the basic rules governing interpersonal relations and sexual identity. It appears reasonable to assume that those individuals who have chosen to remain single and childless are among the most sensitive to these trends, and are perhaps the most affected by anomie. Rajneesh's message attracts exactly this kind of individual: the childless, single, sexually-active adult. Why? Because his message seems to have the effect of validating her/his relationships, and reducing his/her sense of anomie. How is this done? It appears to involve three stages:

   a) the participation in therapy groups which offer cathartic techniques designed to purify members of guilt and to release repressions. By this means, feelings of failure or inadequacy at their inability to conform to their parents/ society's expectations are purged.
   b) the sexual drive and sexual relationships (non-procreative) are elevated to a high status and endowed with religious meaning. The adherent's inability to form lasting relationships with the opposite sex is no longer

viewed as neurotic, but rather interpreted as a restless longing for union with the Absolute/Bhagwan, and as one of the inevitable trials on the path towards enlightenment.

c) the provision of support mechanisms which enable the individual to handle the emotional divagations of a sexually promiscuous lifestyle. The availability of counsellors, therapists and the considerable influence of the group over couple relationships are various means whereby the individual can share, exorcise or reinterpret feelings of rejection, jealousy, inadequacy, etc.

The "New Family" and the "Spiritual Family"

In order to begin to answer our original question, "What do women find appealing in the Rajneesh movement?", it is necessary to look at the effects of the changes outlined above on women's roles in family life. Mary Ann Glendon's model of the "New Family" is relevant to this undertaking. There are remarkable affinities between the characteristics of the new family and the patterns of spiritual "family" life developed in the Rajneesh communes. Indeed, these communes could almost be described as a parody of Glendon's new family.

In *The New Family and the New Property*, Glendon (1985) examines recent developments in family law, employment law, and property law and finds that they are closely related. She notes that while legal ties between family members are being loosened, the web of relationships that bind an individual to his job—and his job to him—is becoming tighter and more highly structured. The "new family" is her term for that group of changes that characterize Western marriage and family behaviour such as the increasing fluidity, detachability and interchangeability of family relationships. The new family also departs from the traditional nuclear family in that it is not a single model, but represents a variety of co-existing family types.

Those characteristics of the new family which most profoundly affect the roles of women are the following: the fragility of the marriage bond, the relaxing of the parent-child bond, and women in the workplace. In describing the new family couples, Glendon notes, "...two facts...distinguish the modern couple relationship....One is that modern marriage while it lasts is companionate, its bonding seemingly close and intense; the other that it is fragile, its bonding seemingly unstable" (Glendon, 1985:7).

Unlike other NRMs which arrange marriages between devotees (as in the Unification Church and the Krishna Consciousness movement), members in the RFI may choose their own partners. Since, however, staying with one person would of necessity limit their power of choice, life in the commune becomes an endless series of choices in which members are advised to live in the "herenow" and follow the authority of the momentary impulse. Thus the courtship stage of marriage is extended until courtship is no longer a means to an end, but rather an end in itself. This pattern contrasts sharply with other NRMs which eschew courtship completely (as in the case of the Unification Church) or maintain a strict supervision over courting couples (as in ISKCON).

The attenuation of the parent-child bond which is another characteristic of the new family is also a striking feature of Rajneesh family patterns. Glendon cites demographic surveys which reveal that parents today spend less time with their children than their great grandparents did, that children leave home at an earlier age, and that their psychological dependency on the family ends even earlier. Rajneeshee attitudes to parenting seem to represent the ultimate extreme of this trend. Rajneesh's recommendation of "absolute birth control for the next twenty years," the sterilization program, the segregation of children from their natural parents within the communes: all these signify a radical rejection of the parent-child bond.

One of the most difficult problems facing women in the new family is what Glendon calls "woman's triple burden":

> It has become common to speak of the "double burden", referring to the fact that the increase in woman's work outside the home had not brought about a corresponding decrease in the share of work they do inside the home. But much more serious for mothers and children in the long

run is the increased economic risk a woman takes in becoming a mother in the first place. This risk factor means women carry not a double burden, but a triple burden. Some women have reacted to the risks of vulnerability in and to divorce, combined with disadvantages at work and home, by declining to have children, in what Joseph Berliner has called "the reproductive equivalent of voting with one's feet" (Glendon, 1985:129).

Rajneesh women, by renouncing the roles of mother and wife and choosing to live in a commune, have solved this particular dilemma. The problem of inequality in the job market is "solved" by the fact that women hold over 80 percent of executive posts in the RFI. The drudgery of domestic labour in the home is not a problem in a commune which allocates specialised tasks to different members, rotates tasks, and tries to undermine sex-stereotyping in work roles. For example, a woman who was responsible for handling statistics at Rajneeshpuram claimed she never once had to make her own bed or cook a meal in the four years of her residence:

> I would come back to my room every night and find my bed neatly made and my clothes freshly laundered and folded. If I was hungry, I could go to the Magdalena Cafeteria for a delicious meal and leave the dishes for someone else to wash.

Rajneesh women by limiting their roles to that of "lover" and "mom" (which is closer in meaning to "boss" than to "mother") have avoided the problem of role overload and chosen what to them undoubtedly seems to be the best of both worlds in family and work life.

Glendon notes that the two outstanding features of companionate marriage, its closeness and intensity on one hand, and the interchangeability of partners and detachability of its members on the other, appear contradictory. Stone, however, points out that the "intensely self-centred, inwardly-turned, emotionally bonded, sexually liberated, child-oriented family of the late 20th century exists under...[conditions which facilitate the]...detachment of family members from the home and from each other" (Stone, 1977:693).

The Rajneesh communes might be seen as offering an extreme example of this trend in marriage. Male-female relations in the RFI are intense, companionate, and unstable to such a degree that the institution of marriage has become obsolete. The interchangeability of marriage partners through divorce, which Glendon describes, has been speeded up in the RFI to such a degree that not only do Rajneeshee enter a relationship with reduced expectations concerning its durability, but actually seem to view a one-night stand as a superior form of communication. As one swami boasted:

> Our relationships are so intense that in three months we can work through a love affair that otherwise might have taken three years!

Rajneesh was quoted recommending short-lived relationships:

> Bhagwan says a honeymoon normally lasts three months. If you're intelligent it will last three weeks. If you're *very* intelligent you can see through all the games and get it over with in three days!

Glendon links the instability of modern marriage to the individual's increased power of choice. She notes that "Marriage has moved from a situation once characterized by...family selection of spouse, to....a veto by the child...then to unfettered choice, and now to a situation where people may...correct their original choice" (Glendon, 1985:32).

Although at first acquaintance Rajneeshee sexuality might appear to offer an extreme example of what Christopher Lasch terms "the flight from feeling" in "a culture of narcissism," there are indications that, in fact, it is a reaction to this cultural trend (Lasch, 1979). Lasch points out the discrepancy between the high romantic expectations with which Americans approach sexual relationships, from which they "demand the richness and intensity of a religious experience," and the "heightened appreciation of their emotional risk" (Lasch, 1979:330). This causes "both sexes to cultivate a protective shallowness, a cynical detachment they do not altogether feel...." He notes that "men and women have had to modify their demands on each other, especially in their inability to exact commitments of lifelong sexual fidelity." He claims that both mystery and a sense of perspective are lacking in male-female relations, and blames this on "the degradation of work and the impoverishment of communal life...[which forces] people to turn to sexual excitement to satisfy all their emotional needs" (Lasch, 1979:331).

It could be argued that Rajneesh disciples fit his model very neatly. On the other hand, it could be said that the pluralistic sexual relationships which existed in the communes did not fit the kind of promiscuity which Lasch sees emerging from the "new narcissism."

Since RFI members share an ongoing commitment to each other to be honest and caring, and since their love affairs take place in a close communal environment which provides its own kind of emotional security, they no longer need to resort to the protective cynicism and detachment of the narcissist. That the sannyasins tend to view their sexual adventures as profoundly connected to their emotions became clear in an interview with one of the female leaders of the Montreal commune:

> You don't understand. We don't just go up to each other and say, "Hey baby, wanna fuck?" There has to be a heart connection. It is very beautiful and mysterious the way the energy moves you from one lover to another. Sometimes I end up sleeping with someone and then I realize it was a mistake; I didn't really feel it. Then I try to be more in touch, more aware. But even if you don't feel right about it you can go up and hug the person and sit down and talk about it. The swamis here are more available than most men. You can confront them, pour your guts out and they'll listen, and don't just walk away. That's because they're coming from the heart space, they have a commitment to the spiritual search, so they are more vulnerable, more available, and not afraid to express their emotional side.

Conclusion

Having described Rajneeshee beliefs and practices concerning sexuality, and examined the statistical evidence for determining the kind of women who join, and attempted to identify their problems in relation to changes in family life, one might begin to address the question raised at the outset of this study: What attracts women to this communal movement which demands the renunciation of marriage and motherhood, and fosters short term, pluralistic sexual relationships?

On the basis of interview data and impressions received as a participant observer, I will propose that the Rajneesh communes offer women five main "solutions" to the confusion and dilemmas arising from changing male-female relations in the larger society. These five solutions are:

1) A female-dominated leadership.
2) An opportunity to reject or gain a distance from traditional female roles.
3) An environment in which the role of "lover" is clearly defined, validated, and "spiritualized".
4) A therapeutic approach to relationships which offers a unique combination of intimacy and autonomy.
5) The relegation of the couple relationship to the public sphere.

1) *A Female-dominated Leadership*

The Rajneesh communes allow women to participate in an experiment with matriarchy or "Ma-achy". Considering that women hold over 80 percent of leadership posts and that more women join than men, it seems fair to assume that there is a relationship between these two factors. Descriptions of the "Power Ladies" at Poona, or the "Supermoms" in Rajneeshpuram, portray women who were well-educated, accustomed to jobs which involved responsibility and authority, and were well-acquainted with the ideologies of the feminist movement (Braun, 1982; Belfrage, 1982; *Oregonian*, 1985). One suspects that these women might feel less at home in the male-dominated Unification or Krishna Consciousness movements.

2) *A Distancing from Traditional Female Roles*

The second reason women are attracted to this movement is

that it enables them to distance themselves from roles which they associate with pain, or in which they feel inadequate. A recurring theme throughout the interviews with women in the commune was their ambivalent feelings regarding motherhood and their disillusionment with marriage and "wifehood." For many of them, joining the commune appeared to be a way of resolving inner conflicts regarding these roles; or a means of absolving themselves from guilt resulting from their inability to live up to their parents' expectations or their own internalised preconceptions of women's roles. For example, one thirty-seven year old resident described the conflict she had experienced in trying to juggle career, love affairs and the possibility of parenthood, and how she had resolved these conflicts by entering the commune:

> All through my twenties I was preoccupied with marriage and babies, but I never found a suitable partner. Then I lived with a man for eight years and the relationship was very close, but he was not interested in babies and I wanted it to be a mutual thing. So I decided three years ago to go back to school and get my masters and train for a profession so I would be able to support my kids but then I went to the Ranch in the summer of 1983. I was talking to Arup about my strong desire for children, and she explained to me that that was not what was happening there. They didn't have the facilities for small children, and that was not the way the energy was moving. I was disappointed, and I sat down and asked myself, "Is this the most important thing for me?"...And then I realised that the most important thing was being a sannyasin. I'd tantalised myself for years, and now I could finally let it drop and I feel I've done everything I want to do with conventional life and now my aim is to go and live at the Ranch. Right now, being in the commune [in Montreal] is virtually the same thing.

Another woman, a forty-one year old former teacher, explained how living in the commune had resulted in her renunciation of the maternal role:

> For a while my nine-year old son was living with me in the commune, but he freaked out one day when we had this group. Everyone in the house was screaming and bashing pillows and running around crying—letting it all out—and he phoned his father and said [imitating a child weeping] "Papa, venez m'amener chez toi." ...I don't blame him, I know how he felt; if I had someone I could call up and say "Come and take me away," I would do it. So, since then, he lives with his father.

For one thirty-one year old woman who had led an idyllic life in the country with her husband and child making leather shoes and bags, joining the commune was presented as a solace and a means of rejecting roles which had painful associations:

> When I read my first book of Bhagwan, I was feeling very desperate. My two-year-old daughter had just died of leukaemia and I had spent months watching her die. We were very close and I was breastfeeding her. Right after she died, my husband, whom I'd lived with for ten years, left me. When I found Bhagwan it was as if I had been dying of thirst and someone had come along and offered me a long, cool glass of water. I became initiated right away. I have my lover here and I will never be married again. I will never have children. When I moved into the commune, I knew there was no other path for me. It was suicide or sannyas.

Several women presented commune life as a therapeutic environment in which they could heal emotional wounds inflicted by their experiences in family life. For example, one thirty-nine year old woman told the following story:

> I had been interested in spiritual matters since I was a child. I was singularly unimpressed with life as it was lived on a material level.... My natural parents were always fighting, always unhappy. I watched their games and their hypocrisy and saw that they were completely unavailable to love.... They weren't married, and first my mother split and then my father decided he couldn't handle me and left too. I remember how we were living in a high rise and he

took me over to the next door apartment and asked them to watch me for a minute—I was only four. I looked him right in the eyes and I knew exactly what he was doing and why and I remember feeling sorry for him that he couldn't be available to love.

She presented commune life as an alternative family environment: "Living in the commune, I get plenty of mothering—the whole place is run by mamas. There is space in the commune to heal; the focus is on personal growth and I feel support.People here are open to love." Her decision never to have children was expressed as follows: "I never want to have kids. I'm too much of a kid myself. I need to take care of myself and fill my own gap first."

Many women expressed relief that they no longer had to cope with traditional female roles:

> I have finished with conventional life. It has no meaning any more. The idea of being a wife or a mother...it would be a dead end, a drag on me.

This notion is found throughout the RFI literature:

> I am just so *relieved* to be on my own...and just be able to do what Bhagwan puts me to do and what feels good to me and not to have any responsibility to anyone else.... It's so much cleaner now, freer, more spacious.... It just gives me the *creeps* to think of all that work of babies and kids (*Blessed Are the Ignorant* 1979:311).

3) *A Validation of the Role of Lover*

A third reason for the Rajneesh movement's appeal for women is that Rajneesh's philosophy and commune life validate the role of lover and even present a sexually promiscuous lifestyle as a spiritual path. Rajneesh offers his disciples a highly elaborated theology and theodicy of sexual love. In Rajneesh therapy and books, the emotional pitfalls of a sexually promiscuous lifestyle are given a transcendental meaning: Jealousy, sexual rejection, and abandonment by one's lover are all explained as inevitable stages on the path to enlightenment. The close, confidential friendships between commune residents who are inclined to share every detail of their ongoing love affairs with each other constitute a support system which enables women (and men) to safely navigate the perilous divagations of their emotional life.

In the larger society a woman over the age of thirty-five who identifies with the role of lover and is sexually promiscuous would generally be considered an object of scorn, pity, or ridicule. The Rajneesh movement, however, confers a high spiritual and structural status upon exactly such women. Women are the leaders in the movement and their sexual expressiveness is not only socially acceptable but is often interpreted as a charismatic quality. The problems facing middle-aged women who strongly identify with the role of lover in the larger society are likely to be social censure, sexual exploitation, emotional insecurity, and declining attractiveness. In the RFI these problems have, to a great extent, been overcome. Sexual promiscuity is the norm; women are encouraged to be sexually aggressive, so they can hardly be described as exploited. Love affairs occur in a group context, a communal situation, so that women receive emotional support and advice from their fellow residents. The swamis are trained to be "open" and "vulnerable," with the result that women do not need to face the kind of rejection, indifference and alienation that their sisters in the larger society might experience in the course of their love affairs. As for the problem of declining attractiveness, women in the Rajneesh communes are vegetarians and physically active through dance and work and therefore tend to have youthful figures (the avoidance of pregnancy undoubtedly helps in this respect also).

One way of understanding Rajneesh women's identification with the role of lover is to regard it as a solution to the loneliness facing childless, professional women in mid-life. A series of articles issuing from the popular media explore the phenomenon of women who have achieved success in their careers at the expense of their private lives, and label the problem "the emotional fallout of feminism," or "the feminization of loneliness" (*Newsweek*, March 31, 1986):

At age 40, most women cope alone with the lack of intimacy, sexual expression, children, social life and the deepening crisis of facing old age alone (*Newsweek*, March 31, 1986).

This situation is blamed on the excesses of the first wave of feminism "whose emphasis on equality sometimes crossed the line into outright contempt for motherhood" (*Newsweek*, March 31, 1986). Another article entitled "The Dilemmas of Childlessness" states that 25 percent of college educated working women between 35 and 45 are childless. These "baby busters...questioned the moral imperative to reproduce and instead forged ahead in the male-dominated work force." Feminist Gloria Steinem, a role model for this type of woman, is quoted making a very Rajneeshee-sounding statement: "I either gave birth to someone else...or I gave birth to myself".

Braun's interview with Ma Mary Catherine, one of the Rajneeshpuram "supermoms," offers a glimpse into the conversion process of a woman who closely fits the "baby buster" portrait above. At the time of her decision to take sannyas in 1979, she was a professor at Reed college and the head of Portland's Neighbourhood Associations:

> ...she was preparing for a trip to Japan, and while standing at her desk she asked herself if this—a desk, office, mind, work administration-was going to be the rest of her life? She didn't feel she was actively searching for spiritual depth, it was just that spiritual depth was lacking. When it came time to book the ticket Japan, she added a few extra days (15) at Poona. After she arrived in Poona and "did a few groups" she came to the realization that she belonged there (Braun, 1984:82).

Many of the women I interviewed were in their mid-thirties, childless, and successful in their chosen careers, and I received the impression that by becoming "Lovers of Bhagwan," they had resolved conflicts between their public and private lives. They chose the only spiritual commune (to my knowledge) which offers women leadership, physical intimacy, an intense communitarian life and unlimited sexual expression.

4) *Rajneesh Lovers in a Therapeutic Relationship*

The peculiar compromise between intimacy and autonomy which is found in the Rajneesh lover relationship appears to have its origins in therapy. In the early 1970's the RFI began to offer an eclectic range of Esalen-style therapies to visitors in the Poona ashram. Therapists from the Human Potential Movement conducted "groups" which emphasized Reichian and "tantric" techniques for releasing sexual inhibitions, and forged new patterns of self-other relating, including a new code of sexual ethics (Palmer, 1987). Several sannyasins I interviewed had met lovers in therapy groups. Attitudes and qualities fostered in encounter groups such as "trust," "being open," and "sharing" were applied to initiating and maintaining a sexual relationship.

Bellah, Madsen, Sullivan, Swidler and Tipton (1985) describe the relationship between therapist and client as "peculiarly distanced, circumscribed and asymmetrical." They quote a patient's view of her relationship with her psychiatrist:

> The focus is really on one person, and there isn't a relationship outside of the circumscribed one. And yet it's a relationship with a very narrow and a very, very deep nature. And so there can be a kind of frankness that isn't possible with a more sort of vested interest. And yet the distance is exactly what makes it possible to reveal so...so much (Bellah et al. 1985:122).

In many ways Rajneesh lovers view their relationship as a form of therapy rather than as a form of marriage. Self-expression takes precedence over mutual cooperation. This is illustrated by the following account of the relationship of a recently initiated sannyasin who was evidently finding it difficult to adjust to a new set of expectations:

> It's like living in the twilight zone—there's never any resolution. Like, it's considered perfectly okay for a couple to live in the same house and not speak to each other for two weeks because they need the space.
>
> I took U. to a restaurant last night and I was trying to tell

her all the frustrations I felt in our relationship—how I never knew what to expect—whether she'd come back each night or whether she'd disappear for days, and I looked at her and her eyes were shining in total admiration. She said, "I love it when you express your energy—I feel all this passion coming from you," and I realized she hadn't listened to a word I'd said, but was simply admiring the way I was expressing myself as Bhagwan says you should from the heart. She had no interest in changing her behaviour to make our relationship work.

When we go to the Saturday night party at the centre, U. likes to go off and be her own woman. I'll be dancing and suddenly look up; and she'll be gyrating in the corner with some handsome young devil or sitting on someone's lap. This beautiful woman, B., wanted to sit on my lap and I was really uncomfortable and she asked what was wrong, and I said, "I don't want to hurt U's feelings," and she looked surprised and gave me a lecture about following my own impulse in the moment and said, if I didn't get centred in myself, U. would lose interest in me. So I began fondling her and she was right. U. came over and started paying attention to me again.

Bellah et al. characterizes the therapeutic relationship as "asymmetrical" in the sense that it "encourages people to see... the relationship as a means to their own ends, not an end of which they are a part or an enduring set of practices that unifies their ends" (Bellah et al., 91985:122). This could be a summary of U.'s attitude as described by her lover above. Bellah et al. also note the absence of moral values in the therapeutic relationship, since the therapist's authority rests on his psychological insight and clinical skills.

These authors also suggest that the therapeutic relationship provides the kind of training needed in a complex, functionally differentiated society, particularly in professional and managerial life, since "...we often have to relate to others briefly, specifically, and sometimes intensely and it is here we need to be 'better communicators'" (Bellah et al., 1985:123). Since many Rajneesh women have a professional background and participated in the Human Potential Movement, it appears likely that they would be familiar with the therapeutic relationship before entering the commune. Many members interviewed described commune life in terms of personal growth or as an opportunity to develop interpersonal skills:

> I have found that *relating* is more important than having a relationship. The main thing is to be authentic in every interaction as opposed to trying to form a permanent attachment.

Some sannyasins expressed the notion that through cultivating intense and honest relationships with others in the commune, they were able to establish a deeper, more authentic relationship with *themselves*. One woman even went so far as to "fall in love with myself":

> When my lover left me I was very sad and I cried and talked to my friends, but after a while I began to realise, well he was beautiful, but I am beautiful too. Here I was, pouring out all these painful emotions, and my friends were saying, "We think it's really beautiful, what you're going through." And then I realized that that was what I had learned from Bhagwan—that I could love myself exactly as I was right that moment; that I could even fall in love with myself!

By "surrendering to Bhagwan" and living in a commune, the Rajneeshee have overcome some of the narrowness and limitations of the therapeutic relationship which Bellah et al. describe. The unique combination of intimacy and autonomy, the compromise between individualism and collectivism, between closeness and distance which the Rajneesh communes have developed was eloquently expressed by a female sannyasin:

> We are individuals who accept our aloneness joyfully. When I feel an impulse to hang on to someone else, I just watch it. At times I feel so empty inside, but Bhagwan says, when you feel lonely, don't run around trying to find someone, just stay at home and celebrate your loneliness! Of course, we don't have a lot of time to sit and be lonely.

Most of the time we are working shoulder to shoulder doing things.... In the commune the emphasis is on the individual, away from roles and relationships. We are no longer identified with our roles, our skills, our talents.

5) *The Lover Relationship as a Microcosm of the Community*

A careful analysis of sexuality in the Rajneesh movement and communes strongly suggests that the couple relationship in the RFI is no longer relegated to the private sphere but is shaped by, and reflective of, the public sphere. Unlike married or engaged couples in American society who, according to Berger and Kellner (1974), create a new and orderly world within the private sphere of their relationship, love affairs in the Rajneesh communes have become a microcosm of the wider community.

The tendency of "world-rejecting" or utopian communal-style NRMs to control their members' sexual relationships has been well documented and analyzed, but if one is to approach this phenomenon from another angle, and ask why the members themselves put up with it—or choose the situation in the first place—there is no simple answer. Obviously, women in the RFI had already enjoyed considerable control over their private lives for roughly a decade before joining the movement, so what was it they found attractive or reassuring about public and collective monitoring of their sexual relationships? They must have been aware of the controls.

Although it is impossible to find a conclusive answer to this question, Foster's observations on how utopias reflect contemporary notions and confusion concerning sexuality might be relevant to understanding Rajneesh women's concerns.

Lawrence Foster (1981) in his study of nineteenth century utopias, postulates that these communities were deeply influenced by the "cult of true womanhood" and the antebellum ideals of sexual self-control. He proposes that their "sexual experiments," which ranged from celibacy to polygamy to free love, could be interpreted as a response to the Victorians' ambivalence towards sexuality. Shaker celibacy, for example, "could be viewed as almost a parody of the literature of marital and sexual advice. The Shakers carried the implications of this literature to their extreme, logical conclusion. If sex was basically a dangerous impulse...then why not go further and eliminate it altogether?" (Foster, 1985:234).

If one were to examine popular literature of the 1970's and 1980's advising women on how to conduct their relationships with men, one might also argue that the Rajneesh solution represents an extreme, even a parody, of modern women's concerns. Best-selling do-it-yourself therapy guides and feminist analyses of female-male interactions counsel women to preserve their independence and to reduce their expectations when entering a new relationship, and to remain open to alternative options. Robin Norwood's *Women Who Love Too Much* (1985), which made the *New York Times* bestseller list, outlines a program of recovery for women "addicted to love" which includes Rajneeshee-sounding advice such as: "Become selfish," "Develop your spiritual side through daily practice," and "Find a support group of peers who understand." Many articles appearing in the woman's magazine, *Cosmopolitan*, counsel the single, upwardly-mobile "working gal" on how to achieve a satisfactory sex life, meet prospective boyfriends, and deal with their fears of intimacy. There also appears to be a healthy market for books aimed at the mature single woman which caution her against the dangers of doormat dependency on the man she loves, and against the addictive properties of sex. Examples of these are: *Love and Limerance*, (Tennov, 1978); *Love and Addiction*, (Peele, 1975); *How to Survive the Loss of Love*, (Colgrove, 1976); and *The Art of Selfishness*, (Seabury, 1981).

The appeal of Rajneesh's message might be better understood in the light of these concerns expressed in popular literature. If falling in love is so likely to lead to frustration and suffering, if men are so reluctant to get involved, if sexual relationships rarely lead to a permanent, committed relationship, then why not renounce all expectations concerning marriage or romantic love? Why not "fall in love with Bhagwan" and live in a commune where women are guaranteed to receive physical affection and sexual attention from the men; where both sexes approach a relationship with identical expectations; where there is no double standard for men who are encouraged to be "soft" and "receptive" and women "strong" and "dynamic"? The Rajneesh therapy groups offer crash courses on initiating sexual relationships, and the communes provide clear guidelines and standards of etiquette for lovers. Perhaps what is most important is that the individual receives group support during her erratic love affairs. Therefore, one might surmise (although this is impossible to prove conclusively) that Rajneesh women are turning away from what they perceive to be an insecure and exploitative social environment to find a sense of order and sacred meaning in their sexual relationships.

7

A LETTER FROM POONA, NOVEMBER, 1989

James S. Gordon

Forty of us, men and women, are changing in a bathroom built for fifteen. Off with the maroon outfits and on with white gowns—cotton and polyester and silk. The bathroom, save for the sound of water running to rinse off the day's sweat, is quiet. People leave, singly and in small groups, and move across marble walkways, under palm trees. It's after six and still warm but the light is fading from the winter sky. White robed figures are coming down other paths, descending from rickshaws outside the ashram gate. Everyone is moving faster now, converging on Buddha Hall.

We check our bags and shuck our shoes, move between the women who sniff us, through the metal detector, onto the edge of the huge covered white marble pavilion and up to the people who run their hands over our bodies. We make our way to seats on the floor. A dozen musicians are jamming on sitars and guitars, flutes and tablas. The music is sweet and upbeat, a hybrid of soft rock and Indian bhajans. Six or seven thousand people, mostly Westerners in their thirties and forties, are sitting in neat rows, cross legged, eyes closed and quiet, or clapping in time to the music, or swaying from the waist up. Some are dancing in the darkness at the edges of the hall. Suddenly the music stops. Seven thousand people, as one, raise their arms and shout: "OSHO!!". The music resumes, stops, and again they shout: "OSHO!!".

Within a few minutes, a silver stretch Rolls Royce pulls up at the back of the auditorium. A tiny, slight, white bearded figure in a floor length black gown and a dark cap gets out. He glides across the marble up the stairs to the dais. He puts his hands together in namaste, the traditional Indian gesture of greeting. He slowly transcribes a semicircle across the front of the stage, turning a soft hypnotic gaze on each sector of the crowd. The band picks up the tempo, raises the volume, and then stops. The sound is delirious now, the noise deafening: "OSHO!!!!".

We are in India, in a fashionable neighbourhood in the city of Poona, a former British "hill station", one hundred and thirty miles southeast of Bombay, at the "Osho Commune". The man on the stage, who now calls himself Osho, was, until a few months ago, known as Bhagwan Shree Rajneesh. Rajneesh, who had been dubbed the "sex guru" before he left India for the United States, in 1981, and the "Rolls Royce guru" (he had some ninety-three of them) during his stay on a 64,000 acre ranch in Oregon, has now decided "to make a total break with the past". He has dropped "Bhagwan", which means "the blessed one" in Sanskrit, the honorific "Shree" and even the given name "Rajneesh". His new name is derived from ancient Japanese: "O" means "with great respect, love and gratitude" and "synchronicity"; "sho" is the "multidimensional expansion of consciousness". Virtually all of the seven thousand clapping, cheering white robed men and women are Osho's sannyasins, his disciples.

The last time I had seen Osho, in the spring of 1986, a far smaller crowd was clapping and singing outside a police station in Heraklion, Crete. Osho and I, a few disciples and a dozen police, were inside in a smoky holding room. The Greek government, after having given him permission to live for a few months on Crete, had decided to terminate his visa. Rajneesh's public discourses, particularly his familiar exhortation to have as much sex as possible, so that one could ultimately relax and become meditative, had infuriated the Archbishop of the Cretan Orthodox Church, who in turn had pressured the government into expelling him.

On Crete then, it looked as if Rajneesh might well be relegated to a footnote in the annals of the New Age. After apparently attempting to flee a Grand Jury indictment, he had been arrested, detained, and then forced out of the United States in a complicated plea bargain on a charge of immigration fraud.

Sheela, the foul mouthed acolyte who had run Rajneeshpuram, his Oregon commune, had pleaded guilty to immigration fraud, wire tapping, arson, attempted murder, and the nonfatal poisoning of seven hundred Oregonians. The commune, once a thriving Utopian experiment, was deserted. The four thousand people who had worked sixteen hours a day for four years to turn it into an ecologically sound paradise which Rajneesh had assured them would be the "womb of the new man", had scattered to the countries from which they had come. Disillusioned and bitter (a number had lost the savings they had contributed, along with their dream), many had renounced their discipleship. To most outside the group and many within, Rajneesh seemed Sheela's fool at best, and a dangerous conman and criminal at worst.

After his expulsion from Greece, Rajneesh and his entourage were denied residence everywhere they landed. When, finally, he returned to his native India, he seemed, at least in the statements I saw, to be succumbing to querulousness and grandiosity, declaring that he was "drop(ping) all hope for humanity and this planet", and then modestly acknowledging that he was the embodiment of Buddha. After some months in Bombay, Rajneesh returned to Poona to the ashram he had first established in 1974.

Over the next three years I heard rumours. Old sannyasins, who had felt hurt and betrayed by the debacle in Oregon were returning to India. Large numbers of new people were becoming disciples. Everyone who entered the commune had to have a recent and negative AIDS test.

The lessons of Oregon, I was told, had been learned. The automatic weapons that were used to protect the ranch, the coercion that kept sannyasins in line, even the poisonings that were undertaken to disable those who might vote against Rajneeshpuram's interests: All were best understood as part of a therapeutic process which Rajneesh permitted, if not encouraged. He had allowed Sheela to live out the dark and dictatorial aspect of her character. His other disciples, who had seen how easily they too could behave like thugs and fascists, had also had the opportunity to purge themselves of their authoritarianism.

Having experienced this shadow side of themselves, they would not be driven to act on it again. No other Master would have allowed such a dangerous and necessary process to take place. In "Poona Two" as the sannyasins were calling it, they claimed there was greater freedom than ever before. The "Buddhafield", the energy they felt emanating from their enlightened master, was stronger; the new meditations even more powerful.

I had seen enough of the ugliness that Oregon became and heard enough of sannyasins' justifications and boasts to be sceptical. Still, I was curious. When the opportunity to visit Poona arose—I was giving some speeches in India—I took my AIDS test and booked my passage.

For fifteen years I had been involved with Rajneesh and his disciples. Originally my interest had been personal. In the early seventies, one of his Indian sannyasins had taught me Dynamic Meditation, a remarkable hour long five stage combination of ancient Eastern techniques and modern expressive psychotherapy that Rajneesh had created. Until then, I had never been able to experience the blissful, watchful stillness that is the hallmark of the meditative state. In time, I prescribed Dynamic, and some of Rajneesh's other meditations, for the anxious depressed people who came to me for psychiatric treatment.

Rajneesh's books too—more that six hundred volumes of transcriptions of his lectures at latest count—had been a source of inspiration. He mocked the dogma of organized religion even as he made previously impenetrable religious texts accessible. In his discourses, Buddha and Jesus, Moses, Krishna and Shiva were thoroughly modern spiritual psychologists, reminding us of what we already knew but had somehow forgotten. All religions, Rajneesh said, "although separate" are one. All had the same basic message: Go inside; the kingdom of heaven is within; celebrate the divinity of your own ordinary lives.

By the mid-seventies my personal interest had become professional. The National Institute of Mental Health, where I then worked as a research psychiatrist, had asked me to explain the appeal of the hundreds of "cults" which seemed to be claiming the minds and hearts of so many young Americans. I spent time as a participant-observer with perhaps two dozen groups—including the Moonies and the Hare Krishnas, Siddha Yoga,

EST, and the Scientologists—but I found myself returning most often to Rajneesh and his sannyasins. All the leaders offered their adherents methods to access transcendent experience, answers to the questions that plagued them, a supportive community and a sense of mission. All had a certain charisma, and all eventually flirted with or plunged into, authoritarian leadership. But none of them was as psychologically sophisticated, as intelligent, as irreverent, as modern, and as fascinating to me as Rajneesh.

Chandra Mohan Jain (Rajneesh was a name given to him later by his family) was born in 1931 as a Jaina, a member of a tiny ascetic Indian religious group founded by Mahavir, a contemporary of Buddha. Rajneesh grew up in a modest small town merchant family, the prank playing daredevil favourite of a doting grandmother. He went to Jabalpur University where he specialized in puncturing his professors' pretensions, won national gold medals for debate and later became a lecturer in philosophy. When he was twenty-one, after years of esoteric practices, Rajneesh became, according to his autobiographical account, "enlightened": "The drop had fallen into the ocean..." he recalled. "I was the ocean.... The whole universe...luminous, throbbing, became a benediction."

Rajneesh the mystic remained an intellectual, capable of giving learned and original glosses on Nietzsche and Engels, and a comic who could present the most absurd or scatological joke gracefully. He was also a spellbinding orator—Terrence Stamp, who was once a sannyasin, told me that Rajneesh was the best performer he had ever seen—and a skilful hypnotist. Rajneesh, changing his mind and his message each day, undercutting his listeners' preconceptions, confronting them with their defenses, was a master of paradox, a shaman, a trickster and a huckster: On Gandhi's centenary, he barnstormed India, attacking the sainted Mahatma; several years later he would advise Westerners who were obsessed with sex, to embrace total indulgence as the path to liberation from their desires.

Rajneesh used the devices of the traditional Master—giving his disciples Sanskrit names, telling them, in the early years, to wear the orange clothes of the renunciate or sannyasin, and placing a locket with his picture around their necks—but he turned them on their head. His sannyasins were to renounce only their attachment to the world not their pleasure in it. They were to combine the materialism of the West and the meditativeness of the East, to be as active, sensual and exuberant as Zorba the Greek and as serene as Gautama Buddha. "Zorba the Buddhas", he called them. They were, like disciples of more traditional gurus, to surrender to him, their "Master", but only "the ego, the false idea that you are somebody special". He was, he said to them, "not to be worshipped". He was rather to be "like a catalytic agent", "a sun encouraging the flow (to open), but in a very delicate way".

I went to Poona in 1979, to experience Rajneesh's work with his disciples—and with me. I did the meditations and some of the therapy groups that Rajneesh had devised to "peel the onion" of his sannyasins' conditioning. The meditations, the groups, the sannyasins, Rajneesh's discourses, the supercharged sexual atmosphere in which orgies and abstinence alternated, the organized chaos of the ashram, all held up an uncompromising mirror to my thoughts and my feelings. I felt my customary defenses, my questioning mind, my self protective judgments, even my fears, slipping away.

I loved and hated and ultimately treasured what I learned about myself in Poona, but I remained troubled by some of what I learned about the ashram. I sensed in Rajneesh a love for power that made me uneasy. And I glimpsed, in some of his highly educated, sophisticated disciples, flashes of arrogance and coerciveness, and an unquestioned acquiescence to group pressure that repelled me. I was especially troubled by the sterilization policy: Because Rajneesh believed absolute birth control, "for twenty years", to be a necessity, and because his lieutenants insisted that "good" sannyasins would follow their Master's dictate, many hundreds, perhaps several thousand, some as young as 14 or 15, were operated on. I was told emphatically that no one was actually forced to be sterilized or denied privileges in the ashram because of their refusal, but it still looked and felt ugly to me, not the kind of thing I expected from an enlightened "catalytic agent".

I left Poona after a few weeks, but I stayed interested in this disturbing contradictory Master and his sannyasins. When

Rajneesh, denied access to the land on which he hoped to build a "sannyasin city", left India for Oregon, I visited his commune regularly. I interviewed him and Sheela and more than a hundred of his sannyasins. I enjoyed the ease and creativity of daily life in Rajneeshpuram. And I found myself rooting for the sannyasins to succeed in their attempt to create a "new man" in an international, classless, ecologically sound commune. Later, I watched and questioned and grew angrier, as Rajneesh remained "in silence", and Sheela and the commune leadership, harassed from without, became increasingly provocative and paranoid; as they and the disciples who blindly followed them, transformed a Utopian dream into an authoritarian nightmare.

In 1987 I published a book, *The Golden Guru: The Strange Journey of Bhagwan Shree Rajneesh* about Rajneesh and his group, their appeal and the paths his and their lives had taken. It was, I thought, a balanced and honest account. I was appreciative of Rajneesh's contributions and goals and the commune's successes, and attentive to the pitfalls inherent in giving over one's authority to another person. And I tried to show, particularly in an analytic "Epilogue", how, in isolation, Rajneesh's self-confidence curdled to arrogance, how his love of power meshed with his disciples' comfort in being controlled, and how he and they collaborated in the commune's destruction. The book, defying easy categorization, filled with ironies and ambiguities, was at once a celebration and a cautionary tale.

Walking around on my first full day, I am surprised at how relaxed the new Osho Commune seems, how free of "security"—of the armed men and women and drug-sniffing dogs who guarded the gates of Rajneeshpuram, the "peace officers" in Oregon who dogged the visitor's steps. Once I have delivered my AIDS test and bought my meditation pass, I am free to idle along the marble paths, to watch the swans in one of the pools or rest in the rock gardens. The early morning meditators, showered and shiny after Dynamic, are sitting in open air cafeterias, eating hot cereal, fresh baked buns and slices of papaya. Soon, the ashram's workers, many of whom I recognize from Oregon, sit down. Everyone is wearing maroon, per Osho's orders, except the psychotherapists who are in black.

Within hours I run into Krishna Gopa, who I met ten years ago on my first trip to Poona, and Subhuti, Prasado, and Subhan who I knew on the ranch. After Rajneeshpuram collapsed all of them lived for some time "in the world". Subhuti and Prasado plied familiar trades, as editors, proofreaders, and journalists. Gopa learned graphic design and worked at it and Subhan, who had been a lawyer on the ranch, sold baseball cards at county fairs and trade shows. Their initial adjustment was hard, but in time they grew comfortable. Still, when Rajneesh settled in Poona, all of them found a way to "come home".

Here they do not fret much about physical or emotional security, or feel the overwhelming need to have a partner or plan for the future, as so many seem to in the world. Their work feels playful once again and their days are full. Gopa is doing graphics for Osho's books. Subhuti and Subhan are working on the commune newspaper and Prasado is editing and helping with the initiation of new sannyasins.

In Oregon everyone who stayed for any length of time worked, some at the trades they practised "on the outside"—business, law, medicine, psychotherapy—others as farmers, heavy equipment operators, cooks and cleaners. Most like Gopa, Subhuti, Prasado, and Subhan were commune members, who received room and board, clothing and laundry, and a tiny monthly stipend. Here, Gopa explains, only five or six hundred sannyasins work. They are the therapists and administrators, the skilled craftsmen and office personnel, the clerks and the cashiers. About half of them are supported by the commune, the other half volunteer their skills. No one is paid a salary.

The commune is now more like an ancient "Mystery School" than a modern Utopian community. It is a place which a relatively small sannyasin staff operates for a large number of pilgrims. Gopa is pleased that most people must now pay for room and board and meditation and evening darshans, that they must keep one foot in the outside world to earn the money for their stays in Poona. It discourages dependency, she explains, makes it less likely that sannyasins will sell their souls for some new Sheela's porridge. If the commune is less all-encompassing, it is nevertheless thriving. The original six acres have two or three more buildings on them than ten years ago; there are additions, outward and upward, to old buildings, and elegant renovations of some of the interiors. Land on two bordering streets has been bought and the neighbourhood is alive with the sounds of hammers and drills. Much of the construction is done by non-sannyasin Indians, as are many of the ashram's menial chores. A lot of money is being spent, but, as is usual around Rajneesh, a lot of money is being generated.

A daily pass to the commune, which allows participation in half a dozen meditations and exercise groups, is ten rupees (50 cents on the black market) and admission to each evening's white gowned Darshan is ten rupees more. The more than seventy therapy groups—which cover the whole range of the human potential movement from aikido to rebirthing and Zen—are extra, as are the half dozen longer, more intensive trainings which begin each month. Each of these costs an average 350 rupees a day, though some are far more expensive. The total must be hundreds of millions of rupees a year, an impressive amount, particularly in an economy where the Indian kitchen help are satisfied with a salary of 450 rupees a month.

Once I get oriented, my days take on a certain rhythm. After some exercise and meditation I meet with old and new sannyasins. We take coffee and snacks and vegetarian meals in the tree shaded cafeterias that make the ashram seem like one continuous outdoor banquet—vegetables, beans and rice at Zorba the Buddha; pizza at Bodhidharma; crepes at Mariam one morning and espresso at the Cappuccino Bar; vegetarian sushi at the tea room the Japanese sannyasins run; and beer at, where else, the German Beer Garden. At night I go to Darshan to see Osho and stay to watch the video of one of his recent discourses—he has not been speaking in person for some months because "his body is frail".

On my second day, I run into Bodhichitta. I have known him for twenty years. Before he took sannyas and left his family in Westchester, he had been Andy Ferber, a family therapy supervisor in the program where I took my psychiatric residency. The last time I saw him he was labouring happily in the recycling yard on the ranch. Since then he has run a clinic and "Rajneesh Meditation Centre" in Nepal, and studied Tibetan medicine. He is fifty-four now, but looks better than he did twenty years ago when he was a wunderkind in the world of psychiatry. He shakes his head, laughing about the Epilogue of my book: "Chutzpah", he says. "Chutzpah to think that you, or I, could judge a man like Osho, an enlightened Master." He is convinced that all the categories of motivation and psychopathology which I have brought to bear are irrelevant to a man whose only concern is the spiritual advancement of his disciples.

I begin to debate Osho's freedom from neurosis, but Bodhichitta waves my words away. He is far less concerned with what I have written than with what I will write. He doesn't want me to slight the importance of what is happening here now in Poona, to ignore the impending global catastrophe—the possibility of nuclear war, the plagues of AIDS and overpopulation, the ongoing ecocide—which Osho's work is meant to forestall. "You have to understand," he begins, "that He (the capital letter is inscribed in every sannyasin's accents, though no longer used in official documents) is using his presence, all the processes and techniques and therapies, to open us up to the energy and consciousness in ourselves. He is turning out a cadre of Buddhas to embody the new man, to show"—he gestures to the men and women around us, Europeans, Indians, Japanese, Koreans, Americans—"that all divisions of sex and race and education are irrelevant." If we but pay attention to Osho's teachings, allow ourselves to be open to his catalytic presence, we can develop a meditative consciousness which may "save and transform the planet".

According to Chaitanya Kirti, who edits the English and Hindi editions of the commune's bi-weekly "Osho Times", his Master's presence is already being felt in India. Kirti, an Indian who left his university studies in political science to take sannyas in 1971, tells me that new paperback editions of forty of Rajneesh's books have recently been republished and that CBS has brought out eight cassettes of his discourses in Hindi and English. He shows me a op-ed piece by Osho which appeared in half a dozen major dailies, and a pre-election cover story—"If I Ran India"—in "The Illustrated Weekly of India", a publication that is a hybrid of the "New York Times Magazine" and "Parade".

This sympathetic interest, I note, is in sharp contrast to the attitude ten years ago, when "the sex guru" and "ashram orgies" were at best a source of juicy copy and at worst an abomination to the Indian press. "Things work out in unexpected ways", Kirti observes; "The American press focused on Sheela's crimes, the collapse of the ranch, and Rajneesh's arrest and expulsion". The Indian press couldn't help but see another example of mistreatment of a native by the arrogant West. When he can back, "he was the prodigal son. And besides, he was so well known, the Indian press didn't want to be left behind". Public interest in his diagnoses of, and prescriptions for, India's ills followed: Nationalism, he counselled, and, indeed, separate, self protective nation states must "cease to exist"; birth control is both "absolutely necessary" for economic survival and the beginning of "the great revolution" for women; "communalism", the ongoing war among India's religious groups, is "sheer childishness".

If Bodhichitta is hopeful about Osho's mission and Kirti confident of his stature in India, some of those who are even closer to the Master are still edgy and adversarial. I have been told that they didn't want to cooperate with me on this trip, but that Osho, remembering our interviews, had told them that I was "a good man" and that they should "welcome" me. Each day one or another of these intimates asks to meet with me.

All of them—Amrito, Osho's long-time British physician; Anando, the witty attractive lawyer who serves as his secretary; and Devageet, a dentist straight out of Monty Python—can be charming and informative. Intermittently, though, they all behave like grade school assistant principals, determined to correct the misinformation and bad attitude of a slightly dimwitted and potentially seditious pupil.

They maintain, in the face of what I have learned from disaffected former sannyasins, and half a dozen law enforcement officers, and in an Oregon interview with Rajneesh himself, that their Master knew little of what Sheela was doing, and nothing of her illegal activities. He was, they say, unconcerned with worldly matters and/or determined, because of his unswerving commitment to "freedom", to allow his disciples to make their own mistakes and learn their own truths. This strains credibility, but it is debatable, and they make the case as well one can.

Sometimes what they say and how they say it are more disturbing. They claim that the physical symptoms of which Rajneesh complained in the months following his twelve day imprisonment—loss of hair, unsteady gait, eye strain, weakness and easy fatiguability—are consistent with his having been dosed with thallium, a heavy metal that is sometimes used as a rat poison. They also suggest that Rajneesh's recent round of dental work—he has had a number of teeth extracted—may be attributable to radiation sickness. The thallium, they hypothesize, was contained in a "tasteless, odourless" sauce poured over his breakfast bread, the radioactive substance in a mattress. Both were allegedly administered in jail, by a U.S. government intent on murdering as well as prosecuting him.

They refer me to several books and pamphlets that sannyasins have published on the subject. But neither they nor the books present any hard evidence for either of these charges. When I appear sceptical, they lecture me about Wilhelm Reich who died in an American prison, and Karen Silkwood, killed by radiation, and the Iran-Contra scandal. All of this makes me very uneasy, and not because I don't believe the government capable of such behaviour.

Why are they—and Osho, who enjoys fanning the flames of these accusations—making charges for which they have no evidence? And why are they making them now, when the commune seems to be trying to accommodate itself to, if not respect, the world outside? Whatever the truth of their accusations, this kind of talk revives the us-against-them mentality that helped antagonize Oregonians and contributed so much to the ranch's destruction. In fact, the accusations have about them the undeniable aroma of projection and paranoia: The only certifiable poisonings in this group's story were those that Sheela and the previous leadership initiated against their opponents on and off the ranch.

My contact with Osho, or rather my lack of direct contact with him, further complicates my feelings. Just as I am finding myself impressed by the integrity with which the therapy groups are conducted, or the openness and warmth of some of the older sannyasins, or the great good sense of one of his taped discourses, I am confronted by another "message from Osho". These are delivered by Amrito and are most often responses to impressions of our conversations that he or Anando have conveyed to Osho.

It's a bizarre way to communicate—my request for an in-person meeting was denied on the grounds of his ill health—and the contents of some of his missives are no less so. He is welcoming and avuncular at first—"Tell Jim Gordon, that now that he has written *The Golden Guru,* he should write *The Silent Sage,*"—but with time he becomes increasingly didactic. He paints a detailed picture of his harassment at the hands of the American government. He says I have "misunderstood" about his knowledge of the poisonings and that I should make "a small booklet to go in (my) book explaining these mistakes". I think that he still doesn't want to see how he and his sannyasins provoked much of what happened to them in Oregon and that he has misunderstood, or that Anando and Amrito have, and that none of them has paid close attention to what I have actually said. But sorting all this out seems impossible.

Meanwhile, I am interviewing the newcomers to Poona. I am trying to find out who these people are, and why so many of them—worldwide as many as one thousand may take sannyas each month—are attracted to Rajneesh? And how have they managed to rationalize or explain away the horrors of Oregon and all of the bad press that Rajneesh has received?

The early sannyasins were rebellious and adventurous children of the sixties. Most were successful professionals who had drunk dry the cup of activism and achievement and self exploration; many of the younger ones were hippies. These new people, coming of age in the late seventies and eighties, have generally led lives that are more cautious and ordered. Many are, to all appearances, yuppies. In the midst of their apparent conformity, they have come to feel oddly out of place. Neither the positions they have achieved nor the possessions they have accumulated satisfy them. Varchaa, a thirty-seven year old American who has taken sannyas a few weeks ago and Julia, a somewhat younger Australian who has just arrived in Poona, seem representative.

Varchaa is a high energy high achiever, a women with a mane of curly hair who laughs easily and speaks directly, a mother whose seven year old daughter is here with her. She lives on the West coast and works as the regional manager of a large multinational corporation. Several years ago she took stock of her supercharged career, her "perfect handsome husband", the "big house on the ocean" in which they lived and the fancy sports car she drove—and decided that "this isn't it". She continued to work at her job and take care of her daughter, but she left her husband and began to look—in growth groups like EST and in various meditative techniques—for herself.

Rajneesh's words "touched (Varchaa) as nothing else had". The sannyasins she later met seemed "so different from other people in the world, so full of love and happiness". It was four years before she took sannyas, but now that she is here she feels freer and happier than she ever has. "What Osho gives us is a celebration of who we are."

When I ask, Varchaa says that she was disturbed by what she heard and read about the ranch, by the restrictions on speech and freedom, and "Sheela's crimes". But she is hesitant to judge what she hasn't experienced, and loathe to condemn a community which is now giving her so much. Her sympathy for Osho only grew with his difficulties. She was horrified to see "this little man, this crystal of peace and love" in chains, after his arrest.

A half a world away, in Adelaide, Julia Scott-Waine was also touched by Osho and unmoved by his attempted flight from U.S., or the revelations about the poisonings. A successful art restorer, she, like Varchaa, had looked around and found her life—the things and places, the food and friends and lovers—"pointless". One day walking down the street, "Osho hit me here". She thumps her forehead with the heel of her hand. "I felt like there was no choice. I closed up my business put my things in storage and came here," with Grant, a friend who had just sold his health food business.

Varchaa was planning to return to the U.S. soon, to live as a sannyasin there. Julia had no idea how long she might stay in Poona or whether she would return to Adelaide, or even if she would take sannyas. Both of them and Grant and Padmini, who had left graduate school, and a dozen other newcomers from Germany and Italy, South American and Asia, told me that they did not know where this adventure, to which their heart had called them, would lead.

For those, like Varchaa and Julia, who are well embarked on careers and experienced in intimacy, the decision to come to Poona can be seen as a sign of what Carl Jung first described as a "midlife crisis". It represents the return of the arc of activity in the world, a pull toward the inner life that has been ignored or suppressed in the rush to achievement, a movement toward balance. For young people pausing at the end of their time in university, on the threshold of adulthood, the decision to come to Poona seems both more radical and simpler. Contemplating the prospect of an arranged marriage in India, a good position in commerce in Japan, or a partnership in a Western law firm, they have, seeing only parental plans and hopes, turned elsewhere to find a prospect that seems to offer joy and beauty.

Many of the 300 Japanese sannyasins who live in Poona (there are perhaps five thousand in Japan) are, like Nikhil, in their mid twenties. Nikhil had enjoyed his studies of English at university, but felt that as a teacher he would be "lost in society", constrained by the rigidities of his culture, condemned to drill his students "in grammar, words and phrases. I wanted," he tells me "to use language to communicate my feelings and I knew I would not be able to." Trying to find another way to approach life, he read *The Mustard Seed*, Rajneesh's book on the Gnostic Gospel of Thomas, and did Dynamic. Little by little he realized that "I could just be emptiness, just be myself."

Nikhil came to Poona on a tour organized by a Japanese Rajneesh Meditation Centre and decided, as easily as a classmate might have taken a teaching position, that he would be here "for life". Every six months he returns to Japan. He visits his disappointed mother and his enraged father, and he works as a plumber or mechanic to make the money that will enable him to return to the commune. Last year he married a Japanese girl who came to Poona with him.

He doesn't doubt what he has done, or the Master he has never met, whom he trusts to guide him. When I ask about the ranch's criminality and Osho's culpability, he tells me he has "heard things" but, that, in the light of his experience, they seem insignificant. He attributes Osho's expulsion and the ranch's demise to other causes: "What Osho says is true" he begins, "about Reagan being against the people and the Church being against life, so why should he have to be kicked out?" And then, pausing, and smiling at me, "On the other hand, I can understand why Osho was kicked out, because what he says is true".

Sunday is my last day in Poona, and Sunday morning is the time when new sannyasins are initiated. I am coming to the ceremony late, my mind alive with impressions of the last week. I have not been as moved by Osho's presence as in the past: The highly choreographed evening Darshan, the shouting of the Master's name, had felt forced, and some of his words to me seem defensive, a bit off the mark, if not loopy. And, to my dismay, the tendency to self absorption and arrogance, the institutional paranoia which everyone claims the ranch has abolished, remains, albeit in an attenuated form. Still, the mission on which Osho and his sannyasins seem to be embarked—the creation of men and women who will bring a meditative presence to all the tasks of the world and to the others with whom they are in contact—seems both vital and well begun. And it does feel good, relaxing, to be here, among people who seem freer and happier and more accepting of themselves—and me—than most I meet in the world.

As I come closer to the celebration music, I try to let my thoughts go, to leave them, with my shoes and notebook, at the gate of Buddha Hall. I sit toward the front, near my friend Prasado, and the two other women who are performing the initiations that Osho once conducted. They are in white robes. Over their heads there is a large picture of Osho. The sannyasins-to-be—thirty are "taking the leap" this week—are in a group. Several hundred old sannyasins—I notice Bodhichitta, Subhuti, Devageet, Varchaa—make a circle around them. All of them are in maroon. Two Japanese boys are sitting in front of the initiators. They are rocking back and forth laughing. Their new malas are around their necks. One falls back on a cushion held by a beautiful young woman who kneels behind him and strokes his hair. The other holds his stomach, and as the music picks up speed, he rocks faster. Prasado is laughing, the band's four singers are harmonizing. The boys look ecstatic. I see their joy, but feel removed from it.

A middle aged man, a German academic whom I have seen around the ashram, comes forward with a grey haired Western woman. The man's face is frozen—in fear of this crazy commitment? in resignation? Both of them begin to sway gently toward the women in front of them. The musicians are serenading them, the singers crooning. Slowly the man's face thaws. He and the woman embrace and return to their seats. I feel myself relaxing, too.

Other pairs rise, come forward, receive their malas and their sannyas names and return to their seats. Finally, two young Western women walk to the front. The skirts of their gowns swing. They are happy in the uncomplicated way of children who have come to a party to play. They bend to receive their malas and clap in time to the music and shake their heads from side to side and laugh. The music picks up, the voices behind me are carrying a Gospel shout: "Praise the Buddha in front! Praise the Buddha behind! Praise the Buddha inside of you!" over and over. Everyone is clapping now and many people are standing to dance and I am feeling the music move inside of me and tears are starting in my eyes.

An then I am on my feet, dancing and crying and laughing, celebrating the innocence of these sannyasins' devotion, and the pleasure of their community, grateful for my own capacity to feel, and thankful, almost against my will, to Osho, the strange host in whose name this party is being given.

That afternoon, minutes before I am about to leave, Amrito hands me the printouts that have been transcribed from Osho's messages to me. The eagerness of his approach, and the pleading look in his eye make me uncomfortable. I am annoyed and saddened and insulted that he is worried about my response, and eager to shape it. What does this have to do with what Osho has for so many years taught about freedom and meditation? And I know, even before I read them on the train to Bombay, that his messages will be compounded of self-justification and pedagogy, of brilliance and provocation, that they will force me out of the sweet state which the time in his commune, and with his sannyasins, has helped me to enter. I know there will be more confrontations with myself and more questions about him. And I suspect too, in this moment of crankiness and acceptance, that I will be coming back.

EPILOGUE

Arvind Sharma and Susan J. Palmer

The fluctuating fortunes of the Rajneesh Movement, culminating in the collapse of the Oregon commune in 1985, are well-known to observers of new religious movements. The North American media has, for the most part, lost interest in the group since the leader's return to Poona. The rapid appearance of apostates' accounts of life in the communes contributes to a general impression that Rajneesh has been discredited and that the fall of Rajneeshpuram represents a "prophetic disconfirmation." Is this, in fact, the case?

In order to assess the Rajneesh experience of "prophetic failure," it is necessary first to examine Rajneesh's peculiar brand of millenarian thought. As Laurence Babb (1984) has observed in his study of *Brahmakumaris*, Hindu-derived NRM's rarely exhibit millenarian expectations because, in Hinduism, time is cyclic. Although Rajneesh is Jain-born and espouses a Hindu model of enlightenment, his system is apocalyptic, however, being an eclectic and syncretic blend of mysticism, psychology and philosophy, East and West. His peculiar eschatological drama, although avoiding Christian language, is in some respects parallel to Christian fundamentalist models, and also relies on ideas and symbols from Nostradamus, the feminist movement, the AIDS threat and environmental issues.

Throughout his career Rajneesh had occasionally dropped hints concerning impending disasters of a nuclear, geological, or environmental nature, but in 1983, shortly before he came out of his three and a half year silence, he prophesied with great drama and precision, that two-thirds of humanity would die of the disease AIDS by the year 2000. He quoted from Nostradamus' *The Centuries*, wherein is predicted a "disease that hath no name" spread through "blood and semen" which will appear in the year 1985 (*Rajneesh Times*, 1985). He claimed that his sannyasins would be among those to survive to build a new society based on meditative consciousness, ecological harmony, and woman's rule. His people, the "red ones," against whom "sects shall unite" (as foretold by Nostradamus) will be the first examples of the New Man—a "Zorba the Buddha" who is "integrated, unsplit," and a combination of the lusty, zestful Zorba the Greek and the contemplative Buddha (*The Way of the Heart*, 1984 video cassette). The significance of Rajneeshpuram within the leader's apocalyptic theory was, therefore, as a "Noah's Ark of consciousness," and "a still centre in the midst of the cyclone" (Rajneeshism, 1984). In short, it was to be a safe haven for the raptured Rajneeshee.

The ideal of the commune was (until late 1985) an important element in Rajneesh's millennial thought. Rajneesh, as the reincarnation of Gautama Buddha, fits the model of the Second Coming ushering in the Thousand Years of Peace. His community, like the Shakers and Oneida Perfectionists in the nineteenth century, was intended to play a paradigmatic rather than a participatory role in ushering in the Millennium. Rajneeshpuram's residents took tremendous pride in their solutions to today's environmental problems. In their utopia, cars drove under 20 miles an hour, the diet was vegetarian, water and waste products were recycled, littering was nonexistent, wildlife returned to the valley and wandered tamely among meditators, every visitor and resident was tested for STD, and "free love" was permitted but no babies.

In the light of these living ideals, the collapse of the Ranch, the disbanding of the international communes, and Rajneesh's injunction to "Go back to the homes from whence you came," represented at least a partial disconfirmation of prophecy. Moreover, for those members who had invested years of "worship" (12 hour workdays) and life savings in what they thought was their final home, its failure was a deep disappointment. Many disciples had undergone sterilization operations as a test of loyalty to the commune. According to Ted Mann's sources, one-third of the permanent residents of Rajneeshpuram were sterilized. Among these are Hugh Milne, Kate Strelley and Nandan who have all expressed regret.

Other aspects of Rajneesh's prophecy, however, have not been disconfirmed. When Rajneesh began prophesying an AIDS holocaust in 1983, and his disciples began using condoms and rubber gloves, this appeared to be an extreme overreaction. In 1989, however, AIDS is considered a heterosexual disease, condoms are being advertised on television, and singles clubs with obligatory AIDS testing of members are opening up in New York.

Since the fall of Rajneeshpuram, Rajneesh has instituted ever more rigorous precautions against AIDS. Sannyasins must now be tested every three months. His metaphorical thinking about the virus waxes with each issue of the *Rajneesh Times*. What if a cure for AIDS *is* discovered? Would this constitute prophetic failure, or cognitive dissonance for the Rajneeshee?

The existing literature on the subject of prophetic disconfirmation seems to suggest two possible outcomes; namely, that some movements survive it and others don't. One would normally expect a movement to collapse when its central focus dissolves or its central thesis is disproven—let this be called the "common sense hypothesis." This is illustrated by the case of the Catholic Apostolic Church which "restored the office of the 12 apostles in anticipation of the imminent 'Second Coming of Christ'" (*The New Encyclopedia Britannica: Micropedia*, Vol I: 957). The Second Coming was expected to occur within the life-time of the 12 apostles. When the last apostle died on February 3rd, 1901 without the Second Coming transpiring, the membership dwindled and the Church faded away.

The opposite case, in which a movement survives disconfirmation, is identified by Leon Festinger et al. and may therefore be called the "Festinger Hypothesis" (Festinger et al., 1964). He, along with others, studied a UFO cult whose founder unsuccessfully predicted the exact location and time of the expected saviour's visit. Following this failure, some abandoned the cult, but others persisted with it, in spite of the unfulfilled prophecy. This suggests the conclusion that "it is not unfulfilled prophecy *per se* which irrevocably disillusions believers, but rather it is the social conditions in which such disconfirmations are received that determine the ultimate impact of faith." In fact, Festinger et al. identified five conditions under which cognitive dissonance may lead to an increase in religious fervour, "the reverse of common sense" (Shryse, 1981: 138-141):

1) The belief must be held with great conviction.
2) The believer must have burnt his/her bridges.
3) The belief must be empirically specific.
4) Disconfirming evidence should occur and be recognized as such.
5) The believer should have support of like-minded believers.

We, the editors, examined the Rajneesh movement in Sydney in the light of these two hypotheses—what we call the common sense hypothesis and the Festinger hypothesis. To recapitulate: According to the former, disconfirmation should lead to disavowment, but according to the latter, this is not necessarily so. What is crucial is "the amount of social support at the time of disconfirmation." That is, were the disciples embedded in supportive circumstances of like-minded believers who helped reach a plausible, acceptable revision of prophecy, or were they alone when they confronted the fact that the prophecy had failed? The former believers retained their faith (though not without some effort); the latter "invariably abandoned it" (Shupe, 1981:140).

Our case studies of the Sydney commune and the Montreal commune reveal that the disconfirmation as represented by the events in Oregon resulted in their collapse. After the October crisis, the top five functionaries of the Sydney commune left. This was followed by efforts to run the commune along democratic lines. These petered out and the commune was closed in March 1986.

The Montreal commune disbanded shortly after its Australian sister, in April 1986, and was the last of the international communes to abandon its ideals and distinctive life style. Its director, Ma Anurag Paras, stepped down and, as one member put it, "We tried everything from democracy to rotation systems, to anarchy." Former austerities were thrown out the window; toasters were back, butter replaced margarine, and couples began kissing again. Men began assuming leadership roles, since Sheela and her "supermom gang" had exploded the myth of woman's freedom from aggression and "power trips." Since its residents decided to close down the commune, the Montreal community appears to be divided into three camps. One camp is determined to preserve the Rajneesh community, and was managing the restaurant (now an ice cream parlour), participating in the Saturday night discotheque, and attending the Sunday Satsang. Another "camp" of sannyasins are living in groups of four or more (rarely in couples or in solitude), and are pursuing their careers or returning to university. These sannyasins say they still feel "connected to Bhagwan," but interpret his message as follows: "What I hear Bhagwan saying is it's time to live in the marketplace, to stop huddling in groups, to find out what you as an individual want to do." The third camp (which is mainly composed of his older disciples) is either in India or planning to go there to "be with Bhagwan" in the Rajneeshdham ashram in Poona. These disciples work in well paid, temporary jobs like renovation, typing, waitressing and stripping. They save their money, and then fly to India and avoid the Montreal blizzards.

Thus to the extent that the communes have dissolved, the common sense thesis is borne out, but to the extent that the movement has not collapsed, there is some support for the Festinger hypothesis. There is ample evidence that sannyasins were not alone when they faced the disconfirmation represented by the collapse of their commune. They were, in fact, "embedded in supportive circumstances of like-minded believers." A close scrutiny of events following Rajneesh's denunciation of Sheela in the September 4th, 1985 press conference indicates that the core group set up guidelines for the reinterpretation of prophecy to facilitate the loosening (rather than the strengthening) of bonds between the individual and the community (Kanter, 1972). In October 1985, the Rajneesh International Meditation University in Rajneeshpuram opened its doors to the residents and sannyasins and set up therapy groups in which participants could exorcise their anger, doubts and criticisms of the commune. There was even a special group organized for the children living in Rajneeshpuram to help them deal with their anxieties at having to leave their "utopia" and return to living in nuclear families. The international communes held similar sessions directed by visiting therapists from the Ranch.

Rajneesh and His Disciples in the "Herenow"

The fall of Rajneeshpuram has not brought about the fall of Rajneesh. The partial disconfirmation of prophecy faced by his disciples, however, forced them to relinquish their hard-earned "Noah's Ark," and the ensuing reinterpretation of the leader's prophetic vision has had a profound effect on this movement. One could argue that prophetic failure has precipitated its transformation from one type of religious organization to another. The Rajneesh movement after 1985 has changed from a "sect" to a "cult."

Wallis, in his analysis of the organizational change in Scientology, diverges from previous definitions of sects identified as schismatic movements within existing denominations. He postulates that a sect's defining characteristic is its "epistemological authoritarianism" as opposed to the "epistemological individualism" found in a cult. In a sect, there is but *one* path to salvation: The organization represents a uniquely legitimate road to truth (Wallis, 1976). Other sectarian features are "the right to exclusion, a self-conception as an elect ... totalitarianism, and hostility towards, or separation from, the state or society" (Wallis, 1976:16).

The fact that Rajneeshpuram did not result in "another Jonestown" and that its residents avoided a violent confrontation, can perhaps be understood in terms of Wallis' typology. Under Sheela's administration, the sectarian aspects of the movement were emphasized, and relations between the Rajneeshee and their Oregon neighbours became increasingly tense. Once she defected, however, Rajneesh demonstrated that he still retained the doctrinal flexibility of the cult leader, and was able to back away from previous sectarian attitudes with face-saving *panache* and to adopt a conciliatory stance towards secular authorities.

Now that the movement has relocated its headquarters in Poona, India, the highly distinctive life-style and worldview that characterized the Rajneeshee in Oregon appear to have been abandoned. Judging from recent issues of the *Rajneesh Times*, Poona seems to have resuscitated its image as the "Esalen of the East," and has resumed its laboratory of experiments in humanistic therapies and esoteric meditations. The Osho Multiversity advertises courses in astrology training, Feldenkrais body work, Crystal energy, acupuncture, neo-zen (*Rajneesh Times*, 1989) and other New Age activities, so that Poona might be described as a distant outpost of the Californian "cultic milieu" (Campbell, 1972).

What lessons are to be learned (if any) from the Rajneesh adventure? Artifacts and video cassettes of the Rajneeshpuram era will undoubtedly become museum pieces. We were told the museum society in Oregon was disappointed to learn that Sheela's "pope's robes" had been burnt, and we are hoarding my copies of *Rajneeshism*. It is likely that accounts of the Rajneesh communes will some day sound as quaint as Victorian travellers' tales of Shaker meetings.

For historians in the future, Rajneeshpuram perhaps will be remembered as the only utopian commune which practised "free love" and yet was ruled by women. This phenomenon contradicts the arguments of various writers who tend to view such communes as inevitably exploitative of women. Witness the words of Valerie Solonas, (the SCUM Manifesto), for whom the lofty ideal of group marriage is merely a smoke screen for baser motives:

> The "hippy"...excited by the idea of having lots of women accessible to him...rebels against...the monotony of one woman. In the name of sharing and cooperation he forms a commune.... The commune, being an extended family, is an extended violation of women's rights, privacy, and sanity (Melville, 1972:188).

It is tempting to lament the passing of the Rajneesh communes and their phase of intense dedication and emotional unity. There is a certain inspiration to be derived from watching a group of people in pursuit of an impossible dream. The Rajneeshee, however, do not appear to feel regret. True to their philosophy of living in the "herenow," one swami replied to my questions concerning the fall of Rajneeshpuram: "Who cares what really happened in Rajneeshpuram? Something is happening *right now*. Everyday Osho is giving discourses and I go to the centre and watch them and I try to use what he is saying in my life, one day at a time."

On the whole, we seem to have been struck by the absence of regret or bitterness in these former utopians. In a curious way they feel they have succeeded, though perhaps not in the way that was originally intended. Many of them regard the "Sheela scandal" and the subsequent upheavals a thrilling adventure or a valuable "learning experience." Some suggest the whole thing was a "device of Bhagwan's." Although many have expressed their satisfaction at returning to a more individualistic lifestyle, all the former commune members we have talked to look back on their commune as a positive experience contributing to their own personal growth and spiritual welfare. Several claim to have established enduring friendships and improved skills in "relating" to others. Only one swami said, "It was hard, very hard. If you had been there, you would be glad it's over too."

One fact emerged from the conference which could be a lesson for sociologists who receive their problem focus from the popular media. Rajneesh's movement is alive and well in Poona. Since the dramatic collapse of Rajneeshpuram and other well-publicized scandals, there has been a tendency for scholars to assume that the most interesting phase of the movement is over. This reveals the reductive impact which the politicized climate of media-enhanced controversiality has on the study of "cults." The Rajneesh have been reduced to "a failed utopia," or "another guru corrupted by the West," or "a near Jonestown," whereas Rajneesh himself, however, continues to dazzle his disciples with his spiritual innovations; and while the nature of their commitment has changed, the sannyasins' relationship with their spiritual master is surprising in its flexibility and strength.

AFTERWORD

Osho—variously described as a rebel, an iconoclast, an enlightened mystic, absurd, anarchist, prolific author, outrageous, spiritual terrorist, greatest mind of this century. . . . He is all this and more, because he is not part of any tradition, school of philosophy or religion. He is Buddha, Lao Tzu, Jesus, Kabir, Gurdjieff all rolled into one, and more. Because he is not a follower, he is a path-breaker. Osho says he is a category by himself; you can love him or hate him—but you cannot ignore him. With Osho you have to take a stand, you cannot remain indifferent.

Meditation, Sannyas, Commune, Rajneeshpuram, the World Tour—these are all powerful dimensions of his work. Born out of the spirit of experiment and adventure, love and compassion, these are existential truths to wake up humanity. Osho declared long ago: "I have come not to teach, I have come to awaken you."

History shows all those who came to awaken were looked upon as dangerous by those who are asleep, the inevitable result being that the awakened ones were crucified, poisoned, tortured. Osho is no exception to this. Seen as "the most dangerous man since Jesus Christ," he was thrown out of the United States and was refused entry in twenty-one countries—most of them boasting of being democracies. In this fragmented world, Osho succeeded in uniting capitalists, communists, catholics, dictators and prime ministers against him. They joined forces against him because he was right.

What has happened around Osho is not a movement—it certainly is not a "new religious movement." Osho has not given any new religion, he has definitely given a new religious awareness. He is neither a leader of any movement nor is he part of any movement. "I am not part of any movement," Osho declares, "what I am doing is something eternal. It has been going on since the first man appeared on earth and it will continue to the last man. It is not a movement, it is the very core of evolution."

Osho is more like a burning torch dispelling darkness, making all directions visible in its light, and inspiring anyone who has eyes to move forward courageously, alone, without fear. He invites us to encounter the darkness—within and without. In fact, he seduces us into becoming a light, a burning torch unto ourselves.

So there is nothing like a "Rajneesh Movement." People came to him, stayed with him, because his very presence created a sense of confidence, a vibrant feeling of joy and celebration. Many left him because he did not fit into their mould. Also, to be with him was to be with fire. To be part of his Buddhafield one had to go through a fire-test. Those who fell in love with him, he calls them his friends, his fellow travellers. They are not pursuing any goal, they are not out to change the society, they are not on any mission. Their whole effort is: how one can become aware of one's unawareness; how one can drop the conditionings imposed by the society, the family, the religion, and attain to one's primordial state of being. "What is happening around me," says Osho, "is not a movement. It is mutation that is not concerned with society, its whole concern is with the individual. It is a revolution in the true sense of the word."

Indeed, as Osho admits, he is "an incurable dreamer." His biggest dream is to create a society of great meditators who have dropped their divisions. "Only such a society can have harmony and peace." His vision is clear: "The world can come to a harmony if meditation is spread far and wide, and people are brought to one consciousness within themselves. This will be a totally different dimension to work with. Up to now, it was revolution. The point was society, its structure. It has failed again and again in different ways. Now it should be the individual—and not revolution but meditation, transformation."

So if one has to call it a "movement," the work around Osho and his vision needs to be seen in terms of an ongoing process. It is a process of change and growth—historically, psychologically and spiritually. Each stage of its growth, each evolutionary and revolutionary change in the process unfolds new dimensions, new perceptions, new heights of creativity and harmony.

I feel that the "Rajneesh Papers" can help us understand this process to some extent. However, the research and observations this book contains touch only the outer shell of the worldwide phenomenon surrounding Osho—its being, its heart remain untouched. Perhaps they will always remain untouched.

Swami Satya Vedant
(Vasant Joshi)
M.A., PH.D., University of
Baroda, India
PH.D., University of
Michigan, U.S.A.
Chancellor, Osho
Multiversity, Poona, India

POSTSCRIPT

Soon after the completion of this manuscript, we heard from the local sannyasins that Osho had "left His body" at 5:00 p.m., Friday the 19th of January 1990. He was 58 years old, and an Indian doctor diagnosed the cause of death to be a heart attack. The Osho Commune International Press Office released the following account of Rajneesh's last moments as described by his physician, Swami Amrito (né George Meredith):

> "My work will go on and grow stronger after I leave my body," declared the enlightened mystic Osho...on the evening of January 19...
>
> All this time, Osho was totally relaxed and calm. I held his hand and started weeping. He gave me a beautiful smile and said, "No, this is not the way, the commune is running very beautifully, and after my death many, many more people will be coming here!" He told us, "I leave you my dream."

His body was taken to Gautama the Buddha Auditorium in the ashram at Poona for ten minutes, then it was cremated on the burning ghats while several thousand disciples celebrated, singing and dancing and raising their arms to shout, "Osho!" In Montreal a celebration also occurred on Friday evening among 200 sannyasins and others who felt "connected to Osho." At this event people listened to the announcements from Poona, wept, laughed, danced. One woman became initiated into neo-sannyas and another received her Indian name.

When we heard this news we considered rewriting the epilogue, but decided instead to take Osho's advice to "Never speak of me in the past tense," and simply added this postscript.

The problem of the succession of a charismatic leader, so clearly defined by Max Weber, inevitably presents itself. Whether this unique and eclectic spiritual movement will survive, and if so, in what form, is a mystery which only the future will elucidate. Osho declined to appoint a successor, and instead created an "inner circle" of 21 disciples who must agree unanimously on every decision. This pattern is reminiscent of Swami Prabhupada's appointment before his death of the Governing Body Commission: an administrative body which has, in recent years, been embroiled in serious conflicts with the initiating gurus over such issues as the financial viability of book distribution (Rochford, 1982). Since Rajneesh himself did not have a single (human) guru (and denied that he was one), it is not surprising that he did not appoint a new "Osho".

There are several possibilities....

The Rajneesh movement in the future might resemble the Krishnamurtians, who also resist institutionalization and are intrepid individualists: that is, it might form reading groups to discuss the spiritual master's transcribed philosophy. Rajneesh disciples might also resemble Gurdjiev students, who have formed "Work groups" around Madame de Hartmann and other old students of "Mr. G." to practise the Sacred Gymnastics and discuss "the Ideas". Rajneesh disciples in a similar fashion might form "outer circles" (as a local swami jokingly called a Montreal gathering) to watch videos and do Dynamic Meditation.

Therapists from Esalen and Europe have been profoundly influenced by their association with Rajneesh and new schools of therapy have evolved from the groups in Poona which today are operating in Australia, Germany, Holland and Japan.

Rajneesh himself perhaps has made the most apt prediction:

> When I die I will be dissolved in my people. Just as you can taste the sea from any place and it is salty, you will be able to taste any of my sannyasins and you will find the same taste: the taste of the Blessed One.

CONTRIBUTORS

Ted Mann has taught sociology at various universities, including seventeen years at York University in Toronto. He is the author or editor of seventeen books, including *Sect, Cult and Church in Alberta* (1955).

Fred Bird is a professor at Concordia University and Director of the Ph.D. program in Religion. He received his B.D. at Harvard, his Ph.D. at the Graduate Theological Union, and is the author of numerous articles on new religious movements and of the forthcoming book, *Good Management: Business Ethics in Action*.

Robert Gussner is a professor at the University of Vermont, and received his Ph.D. from Harvard. He has published many textual and sociological studies in the *Journal of the American Oriental Society* and *Sociological Analysis*.

Arvind Sharma received his M.A. from Syracuse University, his M.T.S. from Harvard Divinity School, and his Ph.D. in Sanskrit and Indian Studies from Harvard University. He has taught at the University of Sydney in Australia, at Northeastern and Temple Universities in the United States, and is currently Professor of Comparative Religion at McGill University in Montreal.

Jack Rains received his Ph.D. in Psychology at the University of Arizona in 1961 and has been teaching ever since except for a year as a post-doctoral fellow at Harvard. He was a professor in the Department of Existential Phenomenology at Duquesne University in Pittsburgh and is currently teaching at Dawson College in Montreal. He has worked extensively as a therapist and became a disciple of Rajneesh in 1979.

Susan J. Palmer received her Ph.D. at Concordia University and teaches in the Religion Department at Dawson College and at Concordia University. Her articles on new religious movements have appeared in *Sociological Analysis*, in *In Gods We Trust*, in *Women and Men*, in *Syzygy* and elsewhere. James S. Gordon practices psychiatry and holistic medicine in Washington, D.C. and teaches at The Georgetown University of Medicine. In addition to *The Golden Guru*, he has written or edited eight other books, including the forthcoming, *Stress Management*. His shorter pieces have appeared in *The Atlantic*, *The New Republic*, *The Washington Post*, and *The New York Times Book Review*, as well as in professional journals.

BIBLIOGRAPHY

BOOKS BY BHAGWAN SHREE RAJNEESH
—By Subject Matter—

COMMENTARIES ON THE MYSTICS AND THEIR WRITINGS, 1971-1987

Buddha and Buddhist Masters
The Book of the Books (Volumes 1-4)—The Dhammapada
The Diamond Sutra—The Vijrachchedika Prajnaparamita Sutra
The Discipline of Transcendence (Volumes 1-4)—On the Sutra of 42 Chapters
The Heart Sutra—The Prajnaparamita Hridayam Sutra
The Book of Wisdom (Volumes 1&2)—Atisha's Seven Points of Mind Training

The Bauls
The Beloved (Volumes 1&2)

Kabir
The Divine MelodyEcstasy
The Forgotten Language
The Fish in the Sea is Not Thirsty
The Guest
The Path of Love
The Revolution

Krishna
Krishna: The Man and His Philosophy

Jesus and Christian Mystics
Come Follow Me (Volumes 1-4)—The Sayings of Jesus
I Say Unto You (Volumes 1&2)—The Sayings of Jesus

The Mustard Seed—The Gospel of Thomas
Theologia Mystica—The Treatise of St. Dionysius

Jewish Mystics
The Art of Dying
The True Sage

Sufism
Just Like That
The Perfect Master (Volumes 1&2)
The Secret
Sufis: The People of the Path (Volumes 1&2)
Unio Mystic (Volumes 1&2)—The Hadiqa of Hakim Sanai
Until You Die
The Wisdom of the Sands (Volumes 1&2)

Tantra
The Book of the Secrets (Volumes 1-5)—Vigyana Bhairava Tantra Tantra, Spirituality and Sex—Excerpts from The Book of the Secrets
Tantra: The Supreme Understanding—Tilopa's Song of Mahamudra
The Tantra Vision (Volumes 1&2)—The Royal Song of Saraha

Tao
The Empty Boat—The Stories of Chuang Tzu
The Secret of Secrets (Volumes 1&2)—The Secret of the Golden Flower
Tao: The Golden Gate (Volumes 1&2)
Tao: The Pathless Path (Volumes 1&2)—The Stories of Lieh Tzu
Tao: The Three Treasures (Volumes 1_4)—The Tao Te Ching of Lao Tzu
When the Shoe Fits—The Stories of Chuang Tzu

The Upanishads
I Am That—Isa Upanishad
Philosophia Ultima—Mandukya Upanishad
The Supreme Doctrine—Kenopanishad

That Art Thou—Sarvasar Upanishad, Kaivalya Upanishad, AdhyatmaUpanishad
The Ultimate Alchemy (Volumes 1&2)—Atma Pooja Upanishad
Vedanta: Seven Steps to Samadhi—Akshya Upanishad
Western Mystics
Guida Spirtuale—On the Desiderata
The Hidden Harmony—The Fragments of Heraclitus
The Messiah (Volumes 1&2)—Commentaries on Kahlil Gibran's The Prophet
The New Alchemy: To Turn You On—Mabel Collins' Light on the Path
Philosophia Perennis (Volumes 1&2)—The Golden Verses of Pythagoras
Zarathustra: A God That Can Dance
Zarathustra: The Laughing Prophet—Talks on Friedrich Nietzsche's Thus Spake Zarathustra

Yoga
Yoga: The Alpha and the Omega (Volumes 1-10)—The Yoga Sutras of Patanjali
Yoga: The Science of the Soul (Volumes 1-3)—Originally titled Yoga: The Alpha and the Omega (Volumes 1-3)
Meditation: The Art of Ecstasy
The Psychology of the Esoteric

Zen and Zen Masters
Ah, This!
Ancient Music in the Pines
And the Flowers Showered
Bodhidharma The Greatest Zen Master—Commentaries on the Teachings of the Messenger of Zen from India to China
Dang Dang Doko Dang
The First Principle
The Grass Grows By Itself
The Great Zen Master Ta Hui—Reflections on the Transformation of an Intellectual to Enlightenment
Hsin Hsin Ming: The Book of Nothing—On the Faith-Mind of Sosan Nirvana: The Last Nightmare

No Water, No Moon
Returning to the Source
Roots and Wings
The Search—The Ten Bulls of Zen
A Sudden Clash of Thunder
The Sun Rises in the Evening
Take It Easy (Volumes 1&2)—Poems of Ikkyu Hakuin's Song of Meditation
Walking in Zen, Sitting in Zen
The White Lotus—The Sayings of Bodhidharma
Zen: The Path of Paradox (Volumes 1-3)
Zen: The Special Transmission

INTIMATE TALKS BETWEEN MASTER AND DISCIPLE, 1974-1981

Hammer on the Rock
Above All Don't Wobble
Nothing to Lose But Your Head
Be Realistic: Plan for a Miracle
Get Out of Your Own Way
Beloved of My Heart
The Cypress in the Courtyard
A Rose is a Rose is a Rose
Dance Your Way to God
The Passion for the Impossible
The Great Nothing
God is Not for Sale
The Shadow of the Whip
Blessed are the Ignorant
The Buddha Disease
What Is, Is, What Ain't, Ain't
The Zero Experience
For Madmen Only (Price of Admission: Your Mind)This is It
The Further Shore
Far Beyond the Stars
The No Book (No Buddha, No Teaching, No Discipline)Don't Just Do Something, Sit There
Only Losers Can Win in This Game

The Open Secret
The Open Door
The Sun Behind the Sun Behind the Sun
Believing the Impossible Before Breakfast
Don't Bite My Finger, Look Where I'm Pointing
Let Go!
The 99 Names of Nothingness
The Madman's Guide to Enlightenment
Don't Look Before You Leap
Hallelujah!
God's Got a Thing About You
The Tongue-Tip Taste of Tao
The Sacred Yes
Turn On, Tune In, and Drop the Lot
Zorba the Buddha
Won't You Join the Dance?
You Ain't Seen Nothin' Yet
The Shadow of the Bamboo
Just Around the Corner
Snap Your Fingers, Slap Your Face & Wake Up!
The Rainbow Bridge
Don't Let Yourself Be Upset by the Sutra, Rather Upset the Sutra Yourself
The Sound of One Hand Clapping

RESPONSES TO QUESTIONS, 1974-1981

I Am the Gate
The Long and the Short and the All
The Silent Explosion
Be Still and Know
The Goose is Out!
My Way: The Way of the White Clouds
Walk Without Feet, Fly Without Wings and Think Without Mind
The Wild Geese and the Water
Zen: Zest, Zip, Zap and Zing

THE YEARS OF PUBLIC SILENCE, 1981-1984
A RADICAL CRITIQUE OF HUMAN CONDITIONINGS, FROM RAJNEESHPURAM, OREGON, USA, 1984-1985

The Rajneesh Bible (Volume 1)
The Rajneesh Bible (Volume 2)
The Rajneesh Bible (Volume 3)
The Rajneesh Bible (Volume 4)
From Darkness to Light
From the False to the Truth
From Death to Deathlessness
From Bondage to Freedom

INTERVIEWS WITH THE WORLD PRESS, 1985

The Last Testament (Volume 1)

DISCOURSES FROM THE WORLD TOUR, 1985-1986

Light on the Path—Talks in the Himalayas
Socrates Poisoned Again After 25 Centuries-—Talks in Greece
Beyond Psychology—Talks in Uruguay
The Path of the Mystic—Talks in Uruguay
The Transmission of the Lamp—Talks in Uruguay

RESPONSES TO QUESTIONS IN MYSTERY SCHOOL, 1986-PRESENT

Beyond Enlightenment
The Golden Future
The Great Pilgrimage: From Here to Here
The Hidden Splendor
The Rajneesh Upanishad
The Razor's Edge
The Rebellious Spirit
Satyam-Shivam-Sundram—Truth-Godliness-Beauty
Sermons in Stones

COMPILATIONS, 1978-1988

The Orange Book—The Meditation Techniques of Bhagwan Shree Rajneesh
Meditation: The First and Last Freedom
Gold Nuggets
Sex: Quotations from Bhagwan Shree Rajneesh
The Book—An Introduction to the Teachings of Bhagwan Shree Rajneesh
  Series I from A-H
  Series II from I-Q
  Series III from R-Z
A New Vision of Women's Liberation
Beyond the Frontiers of the Mind
Bhagwan Shree Rajneesh On Basic Human Rights
Death: The Greatest Fiction
I Teach Religiousness Not Religion
Life, Love, Laughter
Priests and Politicians: The Mafia of the Soul
The New Child
The New Man: The Only Hope for the Future
The Rebel: The Very Salt of the Earth
Rebelliousness, Religion and Revolution

AUTOBIOGRAPHIES AND PHOTOBIOGRAPHIES

Books I Have Loved
Glimpses of a Golden Childhood
Notes of a Madman
The Sound of Running Water—Bhagwan Shree Rajneesh and His Work, 1974-1978
This Very Place The Lotus Paradise—Bhagwan Shree Rajneesh and His Work, 1978-1984

BOOKS ABOUT BHAGWAN SHREE RAJNEESH

Was Bhagwan Shree Rajneesh Poisoned by Ronald Reagan's America? (by Sue Appleton, LL.B., M.A.B.A.)
Bhagwan Shree Rajneesh: The Most Dangerous Man Since Jesus Christ (by Sue Appleton, LL.B., M.A.B.A.)

Bhagwan: The Buddha For the Future (by Juliet Forman, S.R.N., S.C.M., R.M.N.)
Bhagwan: The Most Godless Yet The Most Godly Man (by Dr. George Meredith, M.D.M.B., B.S.M.R.C.P)
Bhagwan: Twelve Days that Shook the World (by Juliet Forman, S.R.N., S.C.M., R.M.N.)
Lord of the Full Moon—Life with Bhagwan Shree Rajneesh (by Prem Divya)
The Way of the Heart: The Rajneesh Movement (by Judith Thompson and Paul Heels, Department of Religious Studies, University of Lancaster)
The Awakened One: The Life and Work of Bhagwan Shree Rajneesh (by Vasant Joshi)
Dying for Enlightenment (by Bernard Gunther)
Rajneeshpuram and the Abuse of Power (by Ted Shay, Ph.D.)
Rajneeshpuram, The Unwelcome Society (by Kirk Braun)
The Rajneesh Story: The Bhagwan' Garden (by Dell Murphy)
Neo-Tantra—Bhagwan Shree Rajneesh on Sex, Love, Prayer and Transcendence (by Deva Amit Prem)
Bhagwan—Rogue, Charlatan or God? (by Dr. Fritz Tanner)

REFERENCES

Academy of Rajneeshism. (1983) *Rajneeshism: An Introduction to Bhagwan Shree Rajneesh and His Religion*. Rajneeshpuram, Oregon: Rajneesh Foundation International.

———(1984) *The Book*. Rajneeshpuram, regon: Rajneesh Foundation International.

Anthony, Dick; Robbins, Tom; Doucas, Madeline. (1977) "Patients and Pilgrims: Changing Attitudes Towards Psychotherapy of Converts to Eastern Mysticism". In *American Behavioural Scientist*. Vol.20.

Bach, Kurt. (1972) *Beyond Words: The Story of Sensitivity Training and the Encounter Movement*. Baltimore: Penguin Books.

Bainbridge, William Sims, and Stark, Rodney. (1983) "Cult Formation: Three Compatible Models." In *Religion and Religiosity in America*, ed. Jeffrey K. Hadden and Theodore E. Long. New York: Crossroads, Chapter 2.

Bainbridge, William. (1978) *Satan's Power*. Berkeley: University of California Press.

Barker, Eileen. (1984) *The Making of a Moonie*. Oxford: Basil Blackwell.

Belfrage, Sally. (1981) *Flowers of Emptiness*. New York: Dial Press.

Bellah, Robert; Madsen, Richard; Sullivan, William; Swidler, Ann; Tipton, Steven. (1985) *Habits of the Heart*. New York: Harper & Row.

Berger, Peter and Kellner, Hanfried. (1970) "Marriage and the Construction of Reality: An Exercise in the Microsociology of Knowledge." In *Recent Sociology* No.2, pp. 50-72, ed. Dreitzel, Hans Peter. New York: MacMillan.

Bird, Frederick. (1978) "The Pursuit of Innocence." In *Sociological Analysis*.

Bird, Frederick and Reimer, William. (March 1982) "Participation Rates in New Religious and Para-Religious Movements." In *Journal for the Scientific Study of Religion*.

Bird, Frederick and Westley, Frances. (March 1982) "The Economic Strategies of New Religious and Para-Religious Movements." In *Sociological Analysis*.

Braun, Kirk. (1984) *The Unwelcome Society*. Oregon: Scout Creek Press.

Bromley, David and Shupe, Anson D. (1981) *Strange Gods*. Boston: Beacon Press.

Bromley, David and Busching, Bruce. (Fall 1988) "Understanding the Structure of Contractual and Conventional Social Relations: Implications for the Sociology of Religion." In Special Issue of *Sociological Analysis*.

Campbell, Colin. (1972) "The Cult, the Cultic Milieu and Secularization." In *A Sociological Yearbook of Religion in Britain*. 5:119-136.

'Carter, Lewis, F. (1987) "The 'New Renunciates' of Bhagwan Shree Rajneesh." In *Journal for the Scientific Study of Religion*, 26(2):148-172.

Cenkner, William. (1983) *A Tradition of Teachers: Sankara and the Jagadgurus Today*. Delhi: Motilal Banarsidass.

Cox, Harvey. (1977) *Turning East, the Promise and Peril of the New Orientalism.* New York: Simon & Shuster.
Drosnin, Michael. (1985) *Citizen Hughes.* New York: Holt Rinehart & Winston.
Eidhamar, Levi. (June 1985) "Rajneesh's Understanding of Jesus." In *Update,* 9 No.2.
Enroth, Ronald M., Boykin, John, Floether, Eckart. (1983) *A Guide to Cults and New Religions.* Downers Grove, Illinois: Intervarsity Press.
Erikson, Erik. (1958) *Young Man Luther.* New York: Norton.
——(1968) *Identity, Youth and Crisis.* New York: Norton
——(1969) *Gandhi's Truth.* New York: Norton.
Farquhar, J.N. (1967) *Modern Religious Movements in India.* Delhi: Munshiram Manoharlal.
Fate Magazine. (March 1986) "The Decline and Fall of Rajneesh." Chicago: Martin Ebon.
Festinger, Leon, Ricken, Henry W. and Schachter, Stanley. (1964) *When Prophecy Fails.* New York: Harper Torchbooks.
Fingarette, Herbert. (1965) *The Self in Transformation.* New York: Harper & Row.
Fitzgerald, Frances. (September 29, 1986) "The Reporter at Large (Rajneeshpuram II)." In *The New Yorker.*
Floether, Eckart. (June 1985) "Bhagwan Shree Rajneesh (Reflections, Former Sannyasin)." In *Update,* 9 No.2.
Foster, Laurence. (1981) *Religion and Sexuality.* New York: Oxford University Press.
Frank, Jerome. (1963) *Persuasion and Healing.* New York: Schocken. Freud, Sigmund. (1921) *Group Psychology and the Analysis of the Ego.* Translated by Lionel.
——(1920) *Introductory Lectures in Psychoanalysis.* Translated by Joan Riviere. New York: Permabooks.
Galanter, Marc. (December 1982) "Charismatic Religious Sects and Psychiatry: An Overview." In *American Journal of Psychiatry,* 139.
Gandhi, M.K. (1948) *Gandhi's Autobiography.* Washington, D.C.: Public Affairs Press.
Glasser, William. (1965) *Reality Therapy.* New York: Harper & Row.
Glendon, Mary Ann. (1985) *The New Family and The New Property.* Toronto: Butterworth.
Goldman, Marion S. (1988) "The Women of Rajneeshpuram." In *CSWS Review.* Published annually by the Center for the Study of Women in Society. University of Oregon, Eugene, Oregon.
Gordon, James. (1986) *The Golden Guru.* Lexington: The Stephen Greene Press.
Grace, James. (1985) *Sexuality and Marriage in the Unification church.* Toronto: The Edwin Mellen Press.
Greeley, Andrew. (1979). *The Making of the Popes.* Kansas City: Andrew & McNeel. Gunther, Bernard. (1979) *Dying for Enlightenment.* San Francisco: Harper & Row.

References

Hansen, Klaus. (1981) *Mormonism and the American Experience.* Chicago: University of Chicago Press.

Heelas, Paul. (1982) "California Self Religions and Socializing the Subjective." In *New Religious Movements: A Perspective for Understanding Society*, ed. Eileen Barker. New York: Edwin Mellen Press.

Hill, Daniel G. (June 1980) *Study of Mind, Development Groups, Sects and Cults in Ontario.* A Report to the Ontario Government.

Hounan, Peter and Hogg, Andrew. (1984) *Secret Cult.* Tring, U.K.: Lion Publishing.

Hsiang-Kuang, Chou. (1960) *Dhyana Buddhism in China: Its History and Teaching.* Allahabad: Indo-Chinese Literature Publications.

India Times. New Delhi, India.

James, William. (1901) *The Variety of Religious Experience.* New York.

Jaini, Padmanabh S. (1979) *The Jaina Path of Purification.* Berkeley: University of California Press.

Johnson, Gregory. (1976) "The Hare Krishna in San Francisco." In *The New Religious Consciousness*, ed. Glock, Charles and Bellah, Robert. Berkeley: University of California.

Joshi, Vasant. (1982) *The Awakened One: The Life and Work of Bhagwan Shree Rajneesh.* San Francisco: Harper & Row.

Judah, Stillson. (1974) *Hare Krishna and the Counter Culture.* New York: John Wiley & Sons.

Kane, P.V. (1974) *History of Dharmasastra.* Poona: Bhandarkar Oriental Research Institute, Vol. II Part I.

Kanter, Rosabeth Moss. (August 1968) "Commitment and Social Organization: A Study of Commitment Mechanisms in Utopian Communities." In *American Sociological Review.*

Katsikis, Melissa G. (1987) "A Study of the Children of Rajneeshpuram and Their Adjustment After the Close of the Commune." Honours Thesis, Department of Psychology, University of Oregon, Eugene, Oregon.

Kern, Louis. (1981) *An Ordered Love.* Chapel Hill: University of North Carolina Press.

Kilbourne, Brock. (1980) "The Conway and Siegelman Claims Against Religious Cults: An Assessment of Their Data." In *Journal for the Scientific Study of Religion*, 22:4.

Latkin, C.A. (1987) "Rajneeshpuram, Oregon—A Exploration of Gender and Work Roles, Self Concept, and Psychological Well-being in an Experimental Community." Ph.D. Dissertation, University of Oregon, Eugene, Oregon.

——(1986) "Gender roles at Rajneeshpuram." Student award paper presented at the Oregon Psychological Association meetings. Ka-nee-tah, Warm Springs, Oregon.

Latkin, C.A., Hagan, R.A., Littman, R.A. & Sundberg, N.D. (1987) "Who lives in Utopia? A brief Report on the Rajneeshpuram Research Project." In *Sociological Analysis*, 48.

Levine, Saul and Salter, N.E. (1976) "Youth and Contemporary Religious Movements: Psychological Findings." In *Canadian Psychiatric Association Journal*, 21.
Lofland and Stark, Rodney. (1973) *Becoming A World Saver*. Malalasekera, G.P., ed. (1966) *Encyclopedia of Buddhism*. The Government of Ceylon, Vol. II.
Mann, Edward. (1989) *The Quest for Total Bliss*. (Unpublished Manuscript).
McMullen, Clarence O., ed. (1976) *The Nature of Guruship*. Delhi: I.S.P.C.K.
Meredith, George. (1987) *Bhagwan, the Godless Yet the Most Godly Man*. Poona, India: The Rebel Publishing House.
Milne, Hugh. (1986) *Bhagwan, the God That Failed*. Great Britain: Caliban Books.
Mitchiner, John. (1981) "Three Contemporary Indian Mystics: Anandamayi, Krishnabai and Rajneesh." In *Rel Trad*, 4.
Mullan, Robert. (1983) *Life as Laughter: Following Bhagwan Shree Rajneesh*. London: Routledge and Kegan Paul. "News Flash" (Rajneesh Foundation Problems). (September 1985) In *Update*, 9 No.3.
Oden, Thomas. (1982) "The Intensive Group Experience: The New Picture." In *New Religious Movements: A Perspective for Understanding Society*, ed. Eileen Barker. New York: Edwin Mellen Press.
Orange Juice. Poona, India. (magazine).
Oregonian. (June 30 to July 19, 1985) "For Love and For Money". A twenty part series. Portland, Oregon. Osborne, Arthur, ed. (1971) *The Teachings of Bhagavan Sri Ramana Maharshi in His Own Words*. Tiruvannamalai: Sri Ramanasramam, Chapter 4.
Palmer, Susan J. (1986) "Purity and Danger in the Rajneesh Foundation." In *Update*, 10.3:18-29. Aarhus, Denmark.
——(1986) "Community and Commitment in the Rajneesh Foundation." In *Update*. Aarhus, Denmark.
——(1988) "Charisma and Abdication: A Study of the Leadership of Bhagwan Shree Rajneesh." In *Sociological Analysis*, 49:119-35.
——(1978) "Shakti: The Spiritual Science of DNA." M.A. Dissertation. Concordia University.
Palmer, Susan and Bird, Frederick. "Therapeutic Aspects of the Rajneesh Group." In *Sociological Analysis*. Forthcoming. *Penthouse Magazine*. (July, 1985) Chicago.
Peter-Horn, Klaus. (1982) "Rebellion Gegan Den Verstand? Eine sozialwissenschaftliche Untersuching Uber deutsche Neo-sannyasins in Poona." Ph.D. Thesis. Berlin: Freien Universitat.
Pfaffenberger, Brian. (1982) "A World of Husbands and Mothers: Sex Roles and their Ideological Content in the Formation of the Farm." In *Sex Roles in Contemporary Communes*, ed. Wagner, Jon. Bloomington: University of Indiana Press.
Price, Maeve. "The Divine Light Mission as a Social Organization." In *Sociological Review*, Vol.27 (2).
Prince, Raymond. (1974) "Cocoon Work." In *Religious Movements in Contemporary America*, ed. Irving I. Zaretsky and Mark P. Leone. Princeton: Princeton

University Press.
Rahula, Walpola. (1959) *What the Buddha Taught*. New York: Grove Press Inc.
Rajneesh, Bhagwan Shree. (1972) *I Am The Gate*. Bombay: Life Awakening Center.
Rajneesh Newsletter. Poona, India.
Rajneesh Times. (1980-1985) Published in Rajneeshpuram. Renou, Louis. (1962) *Hinduism*. New York: George Braziller.
Rieff, Philip. (1978) *The Triumph of the Therapeutic*. New York: Random House.
Richardson, James; Stewart, Mary; and Simmons, Robert. (1979) *Organized Miracles: A Study of a Contemporary, Youth, Communal, Fundamentalist Organization*. New Brunswick, N.J:Transaction Books.
Richardson, James. (1983) "Psychological and Psychiatric Studies of Participation in the New Religions." In *New Perspectives in the Psychology of Religion* Oxford: Pergamon Press.
Rochford, Burke. (1982) *Hare Krishna in America*. New Brunswick, N.J: Rutgers University Press.
Robbins, Tom. (1988) *Cults, Converts and Charisma*. N.J.: Transaction Press.
Sannyas Magazine. (1980) Poona, India. Saradananda, Swami. (1952) *Sri Ramakrishna: The Great Master*. trans. by Swami Jagadananda. Madras: Sri Ramakrishna Math.
Schwartz, Paul. (1977) "A Comparative Analysis of Testimonial Speech in Several New Religious Movements." M.A. Thesis, Concordia University.
Sharma, Arvind. (1985) "The Rajneesh Movement." In *Religious Movements: Genesis, Exodus and Numbers*, ed. Stark, Rodney, New York: Paragon House.
Shinn, Larry. (1987) *The Dark Lord: Cult Images and the Hare Krishna in America*. Philadelphia: Westminster.
Shupe, Anson D. Jr. (1981) *Six Perspectives on New Religions: A Case Study Approach*. New York: The Edwin Mellen Press.
Shupe, Anson and Bromley, David. (1981) *Strange Gods: The Great American Cult Scare*. Boston: Beacon Press.
Singh, Khushwant. (1963) *A History of the Sikhs*. Princeton: Princeton University Press, Vol. I.
Spencer, Metta. (1982) *Subcultures of Psychotherapy*. Unpublished paper.
Stone, Donald. (1978) "The Human Potential Movement." In *Society*, Vol. 15:4.
Strelley, Kate with Sans Souci, Robert D. (1987) *The Ultimate Game: The Rise and Fall of Bhagwan Shree Rajneesh*. San Francisco: Harper & Row.
Symposium on Rajneeshpuram. (1984) *The Development and Impact of An Utopian Society*. Meetings of the Western Psychological Association. Los Angeles.
Talib, Gurubachan Singh. (1976) "The Concept of Guruship in the Sikh Tradition." In *The Nature of Guruship*, ed. Clarence O. McMullen. Delhi: I.S.P.C.K.
The Mesto Muse, (magazine) (September 1985) No.7. Syndey, Australia.
Toronto Globe. (May 11, 1982) Toronto.
Turner, Victor. (1964) *The Ritual Process*. Chicago: Aldine.
Utsava Rajneesh Meditation Centre. A brochure published by themselves.
Valentin, Friederike. (June 1984) "New Religions in Austria." *In Update*, 8 No.2.

Van Leen. (1983) *O is for Orange: Examination of Rajneesh Religion*. Perth, Australia: The Concerned Christian Growth Ministries Inc.

Vaughan, Frances. (1982) "A Question of Balance; Health and Pathology in New Religious Movements." In *Journal of Humanistic Psychology*.

Wallis, Roy. (1977) *The Road to Total Freedom: A Sociological Analysis of Scientology*. New York: Columbia.

——(1979) "Sex, Marriage and the Children of God." In *Salvation and Protest*, ed. Wallis, Roy. London: Frances Pinter Ltd.

——(1982) "Charisma, Commitment & Control in a New Religious Movement." In *Millenialism & Charisma*, ed. Wallis, Roy. Belfast: Queens University.

——(1985) "Religion as Fun: The Rajneesh Movement." In *Sociological Theory & Collective Action*, ed. Wallis & Bruce. Belfast: Queens University.

Washington Post. Washington, DC.

Watts, Alan W. (1957) *The Way of Zen*. New York: Vintage Books. Westley, Francis. (1983) *The Complex Forms of the Religious Life*. Chicago: Scholars Press.

Wheeler, Bill. (1975) "A Study of the Integral Yoga Institute." Unpublished research paper, Concordia University.

Wright, Charles. (September 1985) *Oranges and Lemmings: The Story Behind Bhagwan Shree Rajneesh*." Richmond, Australia: Greenhouse Publications Pty Ltd.

Yankelovitch, Daniel. (1981) *The New Rules*. New York: Random House.

GLOSSARY

ACARYA: An Officiant in Rajneeshism who was employed to initiate new disciples.

ARHANT: An officiant in Rajneeshism who could perform marriage.

BHAGWAN: A title assumed by Rajneesh early in his career; prior to its assumption he was known as Acharya,

CHARISMA: A Weberian term used by academics to account for Rajneesh's influence over his followers. For a detailed discussion see Lewis E.F. Carter, *Charisma and Control in Rajneeshpuram* (Cambridge University Press, 1990).

DARSHAN: Evening dancing celebration.

DYNAMIC MEDITATION: A form of meditation devised by Rajneesh, performed blindfold in the morning involving hyperventilating, jumping and dancing.

KUNDALINI MEDITATION: A form of meditation devised by Rajneesh which combined shaking, dancing and relaxation.

MA: A title given to women upon initiation into Rajneeshism, implying the 'ultimate flowering of womanhood'.

NEO-SANNYASA: A new form of Sannyasa developed by Rajneesh in which the candidate could have Sannyasa conferred on him or her without any formal preparation normally required in Hinduism.

OSHO: A title assumed by Rajneesh after his return to India from Oregon. The word in Japanese means a teacher of meditation.

RAJNEESHPURAM:	The centre of the Rajneesh movement in America from 1981-1985, conceived as a utopian city.
REBIRTHING:	Therapeutic technique involving hyperventilation.
RFI:	Stands for the Rajneesh Foundation International, the main publishing organ of the Rajneesh movement.
RIMU:	Stands for the Rajneesh International Meditation University.
SATSANG:	Communication with the Master in silence, practised by the followers in groups in the morning.
SIDDHA:	An officiant in Rajneeshism who could perform funerals.
SWAMI:	Title bestowed on men upon initiation into Rajneeshism.

INDEX

Advaita 3, 16
AIDS 146, 155, 157
Alcoholics Anonymous 78
Amrito 147, 153, 163
Anando 147
Apostates xix-xx
Arica 58
Attorney General 52, 53
Aurobindo 10

Barker, Eileen 115
Belfrage, Sally xix, 17-18
Brahmakumaris 155
Buddhafield 51, 91
Buddhism 4-6

Charisma xxi, 109, 141
Christian Science 59
Communes 51, 108-109, 156, 161
Counter-culture 19
Cox, Harvey 18
Creative Awareness 62-63
Crete 138

Darshan 92, 109
Deeksha 26
Devageet 147, 152
Dharma 5
Dynamic Meditation 20, 91, 151, 181

Ecology 50-51, 54, 146, 155
Enlightenment 3, 20, 86, 92
Evangelism xvii

Family 54, 117-123
Festinger, Leon 158
Freud, Sigmund 96

Gandhi, Mahatma 10, 141
Glendon, Mary Ann 119-122

Grace, James 115
Gurdjieff (preface vii), 59, 164
Guru 1-16, 99

Hare Krishna 115
Hasidism 29
Hinduism 2-4
Homosexuality 111
Human Potential Movement 19-20, 114, 132

Initiation 96
INS 54
Intensives 19-20, 92-95

Jainism 6-8
Jews 99
Johnson, Gregory 115
Jonestown 162

Kapleau, Philip 86
Krishnamurti 88
Kundalini Meditation 20, 181

LSD 20

Ma 51, 181
Marriage 107
Medina 26, 30-31
Meditation 54, 95
Millennium (The) 156
Membership 21-29, 113-116
Moon, Reverend Sun Myung 108
Mullan 30-31
Mystic Rose 54

Nadabrahma 91
Narcissism 36, 122, 123
Nationality (of Members) 21-29
Neo-Hinduism 14
Neo-Sannyas 49

New Age 108
Nichiren
Nietzsche 141
Nostradamus 155

Occupations 29-32
Oregon 51
Osho 54

Parenthood 107, 120, 125
Peristroika 54
Poona 54
Prison 53
Process Church 34
Psychosynthesis 58

Quaesitor 19

Rajneesh Times 51-52, 161
Rajneeshpuram 155, 160
Ramakrishna 10
Rebirthing 92
Recreation xxi, 32, 36, 37
Recruitment xvii, 35-41
Reich, Theodore 148
Rolls Royce 99, 138

Sannyas 49
Satori 16
Seekers 32-34
Sex 38

Sex-guru xx, 147
Sex-ratios 115-116
Share-a-home 52
Sheela 52, 138, 139, 159
Sikhism 8
Silva, Hose 59
Sivananda 80
STD xx, 156
Sterilization 107, 125, 157
Swami 181
Syncretism 18

Tantra 37, 49
Thallium 148
Theosophy 9
Therapy 38, 59, 100-101, 130-133, 140
Transactional Analysis 63
Transference 91
Turner, Victor

Unification Church 114
Utopia 53

Vipassanna 95
Vivekananda 10

Weber, Max 163
Women 103-135

Zen 54, 87
Zorba the Buddha 142